Tested by Fire:

Recipes for Leaders

with

Metaphors on the Grill

—

Karl D. Klicker

Tested by Fire:

Recipes for Leaders
with
Metaphors on the Grill

—

Karl D. Klicker
Captain of Marines, Retired
Doctor of Education

VADE MECUM PUBLISHING GROUP, LLC

M
Indispensable

TAMPA, USA © 2012

Dedication and Devotion

This book is dedicated to the thousands of my former military students, university students, and the clients of my management consulting practice – who have digested my courses and seminars in leadership, organizational psychology and other disciplines, as well as to my family, friends and neighbors who have dined on most of the following recipes. Many of them have gone on to lead normal lives.

I am devoted to and thankful for my bride, Teresa: photographer, editor, advisor and best friend (who once shed tears over my vegetable stir fry…and then recovered).

And I am thankful for the keen eyes and discerning tastes of my readers, reviewers and editors: John Crawford, Steve Westphal and Julie George; and Beer Editor, Bill Howell.

Contents

Recipe for Success, with

Fundamentals

An Introduction

Why grilling recipes for metaphors and allegories? Because *everyone* knows food. Adults, even more so than children as learners, learn effectively through metaphors; and cooking, on the grill or elsewhere, is a process of transformation. Growing leaders is both an art and science of transformation.

But make no mistake: there is no recipe for creating the "perfect" future leaders (or perfect spare ribs). Perfect doesn't exist, so we refer instead to theoretically perfect...or ideal. As most of the following recipes will attest, there is ample latitude for seasoning *to taste* (and that means for both the entrée as well as for your organization's emerging leaders).

The path to developing theory is littered with *hypotheses:* Propose a solution, test it, carefully record the results, and continue to tweak the recipe. In scientific terms, the grill master needs to guard for **validity** (*Am I measuring what I think I'm measuring* – like customer satisfaction?), **reliability** (*Can I get the same results over and over? Will other grill masters get the same results?*), and **generalizability** (*If process X works on steak, will it work on pork chops or chicken breast?*) Ensure you understand all of the **variables**: heat, pressure, the initial quality of your raw materials, the phase of the moon.

In purely deductive terms, this book is partly the derivative of a brief 18 months working at Enron, in Houston, Texas, from mid-2000 to December 2001. (Enron was good at derivatives…) I would not have written the coming essays if I had not become self-employed post-Enron.[i]

Realistically, however, the entire exercise is wholly *inductive* and pulls not only from the Enron experience but also from the balance of another 10 years in the private sector post-Enron, 25 years in the Marine Corps, academic foundations in organizational psychology, teaching as an adjunct professor for a dozen universities, and 40 years of trial and error experience as a parent.

The end result is a collection of essays offering advice on an array of leadership challenges. These lessons are offered to leaders in any capacity: in commercial enterprises, in the armed forces, government, non-governmental organizations (NGOs) or academia. Adult learning theory suggests metaphors can be an effective learning tool. I've embedded a useful allegorical recipe with each lesson – and the end result is a cookbook for success in teaching junior leaders – with a side of mixed metaphors.

Each of the following chapters has three parts: a *FOCUS* newsletter, a recipe, and a wrap-up designed to tie up loose ends and confirm the Leadership lesson. I've added a *Simple version* of instructions to **some** of the recipes to distill the potential value of the recipe from the beer, the tunes and the occasional river of consciousness. I've updated the *FOCUS* newsletters to ensure the chronological references make sense.

The original newsletters were two-page diatribes on a singularly focused leadership challenge which I had posted to my Laser-Consulting business web site, and e-mailed to some 1,200 subscribers from 2004 to the present.

The concept of *Tested by Fire* presents its own obvious metaphor for grilling and for leaders. If the recipes work – great. If not, test different variables in the hypotheses on your own. I offer the recipes as my *own* hypotheses, from my own 40 years of backyard grilling trial and error. All grills and all chefs are different. Cuts of meat vary in quality, as do candidates for leadership positions.

With regard to food and why people do what they do with food, what they do in organizations and in our commercial marketplaces, consider taking a look at Malcom Gladwell's assessment of "happiness and spaghetti sauce" at http://www.ted.com." (enter 'spaghetti sauce.') ("Tipping Point author Malcolm Gladwell gets inside the food industry's pursuit of the perfect spaghetti sauce.") There is no *perfect....*

I will also note that all references to principles, proofs, theorems, or laws based in physics, chemistry, biology, neuropharmacology, mathematics, or anything remotely resembling something other than Mark Twain, Shakespeare, Ernest Hemingway, or Edgar Allen Poe are only coincidentally and loosely related to math or science, real physics or genuine chemistry. But keep in mind – this is no light read. A once-over will give you the basics, but the more profound meta-theory will take a little homework.

The final pages of each chapter tie up loose ends, peel the allegory, and offer suggestions for educating and training emerging and aspiring leaders in any environment – the real focus of this book.

Caveats: The author further makes no representation as to the health benefit or other gustatory quality of any of the following recipes. Not only am I not a legitimate chef, I'm no dietitian either. What you kill, burn and eat is your business. The Leadership Traits and Principles referenced at the end of each chapter are published Marine Corps leadership traits and principles, incorporated in Marine Corps leadership training – and therefore reside in the public domain. In the public domain, I've taken them to a different level. I've lived the learning (sometimes by failing) and teaching of these traits through 25 years in the Corps and 15 years in the private sector, in winning and losing corporations and in combat zones. In my original correspondence with Marine Corps intellectual property experts (JAG: Judge Advocate General), the Marine Corps asked me to give them credit (done) and do them justice. I trust we have done that as well. My steak and beer choices, leadership advice and other content embedded herein are my concepts and do not represent the opinions of US Special Operations Command, the US Marine Corps, the Department of Defense, Jacobs Technology or Jacobs Engineering, or my neighbor, Tammy, who bested me in last year's grilling cook-off competition.

Vol. 1 No. 4 **FOCUS** April 2005

Enron: Love letters…in the sand

A few years before starting work at Enron, I encountered a lesson on making impressions. While enjoying a warm, sunny, Sunday afternoon, in the middle of winter in Southeast Texas with my daughter of then-nearly 28 months, making castles in her sandbox, she proved once again to be my muse. She and I had been filling assorted shapes with damp sand and turning them over in the sandbox in our back yard to create castle walls, the shape of a starfish, and Winnie-the-Pooh. Her communication skills were exploding exponentially at that age, so every opportunity she had to voice a new word – she did.

She would create the molded form of a bucket, on top of the sand, and announce, "Bucket!" Then she would fill the starfish shape with sand, turn it over to create the molded shape, and announce, "Star Fishy!" All of a sudden – perhaps she had a Zen moment – she stood up and flipped over the shape of Winnie-the-Pooh and stepped on it, pushing the plastic form of Pooh's face and body forward *into* the sand, then pulled the mold away. There was nothing there – nothing raised, of course. It was an *impression* in the sand. She proclaimed, "*Not* Pooh!"

It was the absence of Pooh she saw, I think, in a way an adult probably would not, as if Pooh's full body had faced down in the sand, come in contact with the sand and then retreated to go off and leave another impression elsewhere.

Pooh had left an impression, yet the mold was gone. Pooh was gone. Or Pooh was now an anti-Pooh, like antimatter. It was the negative print of Pooh, therefore...*not* Pooh, but with Pooh-ness.

There is a very human process, it seems, in coming into contact with another person. Don't we often say at the end of a letter or e-mail message, or when parting company with someone we don't see often: "Stay in touch?" Even if we don't literally touch, we each become the mold, each are the sand; we each leave an *impression*. We touch...

Not-Pooh after not-Pooh, if my daughter doesn't like the results she can make another impression in the sand. And another. And another. She can make not-Pooh all afternoon in her quest for a perfect impression. In real life the impression is what's left after the communication. No matter how we communicate – by touch, body language, verbally, electronically, in black and white pictures or cinematically rich color, through music, dance, sports, social media, graphic art or otherwise, all human interaction is marked by communication, leaving an impression.

Rain comes; and as with love letters on the beach, the sandbox soon forgets both Pooh and not-Pooh impressions. But the customer remembers those impressions. The employee remembers that communication. Every communication, every touch, is a transaction. It's where the organization, and the people who are individuals, but collectively make up the organization – intersect.

Enron made an impression on people. For those seeking employment with the then-rising star, part of the impression created by Enron was the reality that Enron had been named "Most Innovative Company" in America by

Fortune magazine several years running. And it was! Enron was *amazingly* innovative. Among other things, Enron blazed new trails in the global trade in commodities and risk derivatives, bending rules and re-writing business play books.

Enron also made an impression with above-market salaries and bonuses. This may be part of what led to Enron's implosion. Silver Porsches and red Ferraris in the parking garage were impressive. Bonus babies made impressive million-dollar bonuses by inking billion-dollar contracts. The Enron tower downtown Houston was impressive. Well into early 2001, Enron's market cap was impressive, and Enron impressed customers and clients alike with superior innovations. Enron spoke in dollars. Loudly and impressively. Enron made an impression.

In time, Enron's focus shifted from customer service to *stock price*. When you focus on one thing, it's nearly impossible to focus on something else. You either can't see it, or it's out of focus. Enron posted its stock price at the entrance to the grand lobby. Folklore about stock splits was printed on the paper cups by the water coolers. Enron offered employees soon-worthless stock options as placebos for *Respect, Integrity, Communication & Excellence* (*R.I.C.E.*: a nod to CEO Ken Lay's alma mater Rice University) when Enron announced a $1.1B charge in mid-October, 2001. By then, Enron's stock had fallen to $33/share, a third of the mid-2000 value. Enron closed at about 8 cents on the last trading day of November 2001.

Enron's focus on stock price and off-balance sheet deals designed to impress investors – in order to keep stock value buoyed – meant a *lack* of focus on customers and employees. There's no room for debate on this. Nowhere to wiggle. Huge private sector failures prove the point: You can't *make* a profit.

You can *realize* a profit, but profit isn't a *thing* you can manufacture; it's a result – a derivative of revenue, which is a derivative of customer satisfaction, which in turn is a derivative of employees who are trained, nurtured and treated like leaders in their own right. The master of derivatives had defined – derived – its own defeat. Read your Drucker. Understand the real derivatives…Understand the *foundations* of running a real business.

You simply cannot go to your workshop and synthesize a "profit…" only the *means* to generate revenue. If no one is interested in your product or service, despite a barrage of advertising, you have no customers. No market – no revenue. Even if you generate revenue, you still have to manage the internal workings of your organization to squeeze out a profit. Sure you have stock holders who own a portion of the company, but they too need to focus on quality and customer service. As stockholders, they should be more than interested in how you manage the company.

Focus is about customers and quality, employee safety and job satisfaction, efficiency and durability of capital equipment. Keeping team members focused on everything *BUT* profit is the counterintuitive role of the leader, every leader, including the CEO. Enron focused on profit, but tracing that profit back to its origin through a chain of derivatives is like going back to find *love letters in the sand*.

There was a time when Enron was the symbol of success, when Enron mattered. Now it doesn't.

Pooh; not-Pooh. Matter; anti-matter.

Enron today; gone tomorrow.

Recipe for Success, with Foundations

Perhaps obviously, the words *fundamental* and *foundation* have a common root in the Latin *fundamentum.* The first item on the menu (below) serves as a foundation for the remaining dialog on the fundamentals of leadership and a discussion on the wisdom of protecting your investments: the grill…and that new class of junior leaders in your care.

After watching too many of my $250 to $500 barbeque grills morph into puddles of iron oxide over the past 35 years, the decision to put three weekends and roughly $1000 into a shelter was easy to justify as a prophylactic enterprise.

The following plan is only a hypothesis; modify according to the space you have, your budget, climate, and other needs. The ultimate goal is to keep my gas grill out of the weather, but the added benches, a beer bottle opener and cooler make the shelter a genuine meeting place (bring your own cigars) *as well as* a Grilling Pagoda or Grilling Studio.

It won't make you a better grill master, but it will keep you dry if the rains come while cooking and keep the grill drier between grilling episodes. Because this is an open shelter, you have the option to add weather guards – like roll-up Roman shades on the back or sides, for example.

BILL OF MATERIALS

(All lumber is based on prices for pressure-treated pine at a national do-it-yourself lumber, hardware, tools, electrical, plumbing, gardening, etc. kind of store, in Florida, in January, 2011. Adjust accordingly.)

PAD (approx 8-foot X 10-foot footprint)

You can do without this if you're seeking to cut costs. I built my pad, with paving stones, because my back yard slopes into a tropical jungle and I needed to extend a flat section of yard with a small retaining wall to accommodate the overhead structure and provide enough surface area to support the DOMINATOR 5000 grill I received for Christmas. You may be able to scrape the grass off an 8-foot by 10-foot section of yard, if you have a flat landscape, buy enough pea gravel or dirt and avoid the costs for 4X4s, rebar, paving stones and paving joint sand, and save $350.

The Pad

Retaining wall – 16 4X4 10' @ $10.97 – 175.52

Rebar – 8 #4, 4' @ 3.15 – 25.20

Clean fill dirt – 4 yards @ 15 – 60.00

Paver joint sand – 40-lb. pail – 19.97

Grilling Studio Shelter

Corner verticals – 4 4X6 12' @ $19.97 ea – 79.88

Rear center vertical – 1 4X4 10' @ 10.97 – 10.97

Rafters and cross beams – 12 2X6 10' @ 5.97 – 71.64

Front and rear headers; one rear horizontal stabilizer – 3 2X6 12' @ 6.97 – 20.91

Optional Benches

Bench seats; back rests – both sides 8 2X8 10' @ $6.97 – 55.76

(use leftovers from corner 4X6's as legs for bench seats: approx. 20 inches high)

Hardware – for the shelter

2.75X1-inch gusset angles – 24 @ $0.77 – $18.48

2X6 hangers – 10 @ 1.48 – 14.80

2X10-foot tin roof sheets (120 sq. ft.) ~ 6 @ 19.95 ea – 119.70

Box of 100 Sheet to Wood Screws #10-16X1 – 1.97

2.5-inch exterior screws – 2# @ 8.47 – 16.94

3-inch common nails – 2# @ 3.47 – 6.94

Carriage bolts – 8 8"X 3/8" @ 2.65 ea – 21.20

Nuts for carriage bolts – 8 @ .22 ea – 1.76

Washers for carriage bolts – 8 @ .38 ea – 3.04

Pea gravel – 40-pound bag – 3.67

Tinted water sealer – gallon – 27.95

Total: $855.20

We also added a circuit to our circuit box in the garage and ran power to a GFCI box on one corner vertical post of the grilling pagoda – to power a pair of external lamps and a dual outlet (for tunes, a fan or the rotisserie). An additional expense (not included in this total), but tied to running power to external lights for our swimming pool.

The overhead rafters also provide excellent small storage space for accessories: nail a piece of ¼ inch plywood to two overhead rafters to make a small 2X6 ceiling portion an upside-down "drawer." And – with a one-inch diameter pipe and some hooks in the rafters, you can hang grilling tools.

Recipe for Success, with Integrity

No. I'm not going to litter this allegory with sophomoric symbolism and I'm also not going to build this thing for you. You figure it out; I've already done 90 percent of the work. And – you already know your junior leaders need a solid foundation and that sometimes you need to provide cover for them. Allegories are supposed to be *full* of symbolism. Sophomores get more detail and explanation; seniors get variables and the opportunity to form their own hypotheses.

What I *will* offer in this book are clues.

The original story (the Enron-focused essay of this first chapter) discusses the impressions Enron made in the business world. Ten years on, the lasting impressions from Enron are of a company steeped in deception. While these historical impressions are both predictable and understandable (conflict sells newspapers), they are neither universally true nor fair. Many good and honest people worked at Enron, completely focused on helping corporate clients save buckets of money – on energy costs, for example.

But there is another emblematic look at this that follows from the original essay and the Grilling Studio. It doesn't matter if you take it from *The Three Little Pigs* or the Bible (Matthew 7: 24). A house built on a solid foundation will not fail.

The *structural integrity* of this Grilling Studio relies on 4X6 corner verticals (4X4s can twist and warp. 4X6s are less inclined to do so.); sinking the 4X6 corner verticals two feet deep with tamped earth, or better yet – a concrete footing; and the interlocking headers, rafters and crossbeams, with gusset angles screwed in at two of the four corners of each of the intersecting rafters.

Clue

This structure has a roofline drop from 7 feet high to 6 ½ feet from front to back. In order to cut your 12-foot 4X6 posts while they are still on the horizontal, you'll need to use some algebra and mark off the rectangle for the internal footprint of the studio – so you know where the corner posts will stand in your yard. Depending on the medium you're working with (the composition of the soil in your back yard), chalk line or spray paint may work. Posts with string (sticks or 8-inch nails for your rain gutters) is the best alternative and allows you to move your corners so you can check for square corners and symmetry. With your external perimeters marked, use a post-hole digger to remove earth about 26-28 inches deep for each corner post. (deeper if it's loose, sandy soil). Pour 2-4 inches of pea gravel in each hole, a little at a time, to assist with this process. Pea gravel in the hole, under the posts, will help drain moisture (whether you use concrete footings or not), and while you're adjusting the verticals – you can add or remove a little at a time to one hole or the other. After standing the 4X6s in the holes (with pea gravel in the bottom), mark <2 feet> clearly on what will be the earth-/yard-level bottom of the vertical posts once the base of each post is in the hole. Those marks should end up, eventually, at ground level (yard-level).

With an accomplice holding a post vertical in the hole, measure *from the ground up* and mark off 7 feet for the front; 6 ½ feet for the rear. Once you lift the post out of the hole to lay it horizontal, you can first cut the top off to make a 7-foot or 6 ½ foot corner vertical post, then cut a notch for the 2X6 header to rest on (running horizontally from front corner to front corner or back corner to back corner). For the first-timers in the audience, that notch would be 1.75 inches by 5.5 inches for a finished 2X6 horizontal header board.

Once you have your 7-foot or 6.5-foot verticals and the notches for your horizontal header beams, stand the front corner posts in the left and right pits and reach the headers into place. Use a level to determine if you need to raise one side or the other. You may need a ladder. If an adjustment is necessary, pull the header down, and with your accomplice if necessary – lift a vertical beam and drop some pea gravel into the hole, or conversely – remove a bit. (Wearing good leather gloves, lift and drop the post into the hole a couple of times to ensure it's seated. Re-position the header and check again with the level.)

Before you make your final decisions on securing the verticals, you may want to *mark and drill holes for the carriage bolts* (for the crossbeam header: two galvanized bolts with washers and nuts at the intersection of each vertical and header corner). If you get a good seat but you're off a fraction, you can also adjust your horizontals with small shims in the notched 4X6; it will be the carriage bolts that hold the cross beams in position horizontally – once you have your verticals seated.

With the headers leveled and the vertical posts seated, remove the headers (that are balancing on the notches) and firm up the vertical corner posts. At the minimum you need to pour in a little dark earth at a time and use a tamping pole. A 2X4 will work, as will a solid 5-foot long 2-inch diameter pole (a branch cut from a Brazilian Pepper tree sawed off square at the bottom.) Tamp rich, dark earth all around until you reach ground level. Or, use wet concrete and make a firmer decision on how to secure the verticals.

Next: Install the carriage bolts after the vertical posts are fixed in place. (If using wet concrete – wait overnight for the concrete to cure before proceeding to the next steps.) With either tamped earth or concrete, check for vertical on all four sides with a level until the post is firm and fixed. You've just completed your investment in structural integrity.

On that second weekend, that next Saturday morning – you're ready to sink the rear verticals and build the rafters...and consider the fundamentals of teaching junior leaders. I'm confident you'll figure it out. It's a trial and error process.

And now – the book following is designed to diminish the frustration of trial and error while offering some grilling tips and some allegories and metaphors the reader might use as teaching points and conversation starters. You can have all of the Leadership Traits and demonstrate all of the Leadership Principles, but if you don't have...or demonstrate...with (structural) *INTEGRITY*, all of these are for naught.

Marine Corps Leadership Traits
Integrity; Dependability

Vol. 1 No. 6 **FOCUS** June 2005

In search of
the Wizard of Osmosis

Daughter recently asked, "Daddy, what would have happened if Dorothy had taken the Red Brick Road?"

"Well, Little One, I suppose that either she would have *never* accomplished her goal of finding the Wizard, or…she might have accomplished her goal to find the Wizard but had different adventures."

"Daddy…"

"Yes…?"

"Dorothy's real goal wasn't to find the Wizard. Her goal was to get back to Kansas."

Eight-year-olds!

Seems there's more than enough fodder in *The Wizard of Oz*, 66 years on, to fuel discussions relevant to contemporary organizations. There's enough of a model in fact to feed a book on "individual and organizational accountability" (The OZ Principleⁱⁱ). Still an excellent read.

Yet there is even more than the necessity of taking the first step (and starting on the right road), having the heart to own the problem, the courage to face it and the wisdom to solve it. There is more than the realization that Kansas is a strategic objective, the Wizard a tactical maneuver and that the Scarecrow, Tin Man, Lion and Good Witch are force multipliers.

What we've missed is Dorothy's *orientation* to the land Over the Rainbow. Starting with the Munchkins, and Good Witch Glinda's coming and going (in the 1939 film), Dorothy has some trouble adjusting to a culture far different from gray, predictable Kansas. The people who live there take it all for granted; to Dorothy, it's all new and strange. No one, it seems, provides Dorothy with an employee handbook or visitor's guide. It's all discovery, and the brief orientation – once inside the gates of OZ – is segued with a horse of a different color to the nearly immediate interruption by the Wicked Witch of the West. And then for Dorothy and crew, the reverie is gone and it's time to get back to work.

An organization's culture is not unlike a membrane – people enter; people leave, like water being absorbed through a permeable membrane in the process of reverse osmosis. (People come and go so quickly around here!) But is it a totally permeable membrane? Like Dorothy – do we totally pass through the membrane into the new culture? The process of being absorbed and accepted in a new organization can be quick or slow, painless or painful, complete...or never quite so. Dorothy eventually felt welcome in the Land of Oz, but in the end she was focused on home, and Oz was not home.

In our organizations, we have people who show up, work, go home – never feeling like they belong to the team, wondering if they are relevant. You may see it in their faces; you may detect it in their work, or how they interact (or not) with fellow team members. It comes down to a question: How can you hope for teamwork from your team members if you don't have commitment from them? In defense of the lone employee, we live in a generation of uncertainty, with mergers and acquisitions, off-shoring of jobs, and commercial bankruptcies wiping out pension plans. How can I feel committed to my company if I don't feel it's committed to me? Dorothy, the Scarecrow, the Tin Man and the Lion were bound in teamwork by something bigger than themselves – the realization that they would fail individually and thus were faithful to each other's success.

On the other hand, the front-line supervisors, managers and even directors are caught in the middle. That's you. Corporate decisions are generally out of your hands (except in very small companies), and the information needed to feed your team members solid, confident communication they can trust – just isn't there. Seems we have a two-way yellow-brick road.

It's time for *pull* and *push*. Unless you *are* the president and CEO, there's no limit to the ways you can ask someone senior to you: "What's your vision for the coming quarter? Year? Five years?" PULL that information from the person who signs your performance appraisal. Ask questions. Develop goals. Shape the vision for your own team and PUSH.

Move next to your company or team orientation. Is it 30 minutes of signing the W-4 form and filling out health and dental plan paperwork, then off to the cubicle farm or the plant floor? Is it a day full of meeting people, understanding the BIG picture, the inputs and outputs and relevancy of the job? Is it a week-long event, with all of this *plus* the history, values and culture of the company? Do you have a "Standard Operating Procedure?" Has someone written "The Absolute

Essential Things You Need to Know During the First Four Weeks On The Job?"

An interesting model comes from The Container Store – six years in the top 15 on *Fortune Magazine's* "Best Places to Work" list. The Container Store *invests* more than 230 hours in training for <u>first-year</u> employees, about *30 times* their industry average. The results show up in commitment (retention rates), profitability, customer satisfaction and other ways.

The Container Store isn't the only company that "gets it." Southwest Airlines, W. L. Gore, 3M and others perform the seemingly impossible – pulling strangers from another world, through the membrane and into their own, making them feel like part of a family. Another example, outside of corporate America, is the Marine Corps. But that's another essay. As for *reverse* osmosis and passing through semi-permeable membranes, 10 years into retirement, as a salty 50-year-old Captain, I've accepted a recall to active duty in the Marine Corps.

(Salty? That was 2005. In 2013 – perhaps more "seasoned...")

Semper Fidelis.

Recipe for Success, with Beer Can Chicken

As for pushing seasons and old salts through membranes, the comprehensive Web search reveals an interesting debate – bordering on American folklore: Who invented the beer can chicken technique? Some of the entertainment in this is browsing the Internet, looking for the origins of this innovation. Some of the entertainment is wrapped around the boasting, some around the basting, and much around the best beer to leave in the can (a honey wheat Autumn brew?) But what it gets down to is that behind the title of *Beer Can Chicken* there is a process or technique.

In this case – the process is OSMOSIS. And, what better way to infuse a roast chicken than through osmosis? The goal, of course, is to get both the moisture (and flavor) resident in the beer can (beer or not) and the flavor in the external seasonings (we'll get to that) into the chicken.

The people's encyclopedia says: "A semi-permeable membrane…is a membrane that will allow certain molecules or ions to pass through it by diffusion. The rate of passage depends on the pressure, concentration and temperature of the molecules or solutes on either side, as well as the permeability of the membrane to each solute."[iii]

There you have it: all of the skin on the inside cavity or outside of your intact poultry is a membrane; the molecules or ions we're interested in are the flavors in suspension in the fluid in the beer (grains, hops, honey, chocolate, fruits, barley, etc.). Temperature speaks for itself, and "pressure" speaks to cooking with the grill lid closed (more pressure than with the grill lid open). And – more robust beers have a greater concentration of ions.

First: Since we're innovating, situate four summer wheat beers on ice and keep two out – one for yourself and one for your Grill Friend. Crank up some Willie Nelson traveling songs.

Second: The platform. It's possible to roast a chicken with a beer can up its butt with nothing but the beer can. I've tried it. Think in terms of the beer can and the chicken legs being three legs of a stool. But... there are better alternatives. Numerous (inexpensive) commercial devices are available for this process – ranging from around $5 to something approaching $20. The general idea is to provide a platform or container for the beer can – that helps the chicken stand on two legs. (No endorsements. Do a search. I bought two for $5 each at a "leftover wholesale" company with a national footprint.)

Third: The Beer. My personal beer aficionado, Bill (for whom my barley and hops respect goes back decades), recommends:

Whenever you're cooking with beer, the first rule to remember is that cooking tends to concentrate flavors, which means that you want to stay away from very hoppy beers. An IPA that tastes great in a glass, when reduced by cooking, will produce a sauce that's too bitter to be enjoyable.[iv]

The choice of beer for your Beer Can Chicken should also reflect what else you're doing to the chicken. Are you using a spice rub or some other strong seasoning? If so, you'll want a stronger beer to stand up to those "big" flavors. In order of increasing intensity, here are my suggestions. Note: not all of these may be available in cans; you may have to buy them in bottles and improvise.

Wheat Beer: This could be a German Hefeweizen, a Belgian Wit, or an American Wheat. They all have a light, delicate flavor that will complement that of the chicken. An easily obtainable commercial example would be an American Wheat from the Rockies.

Amber Ale: This beer has more maltiness and less fruitiness than a Wheat beer, but is still relatively delicate and not overly bitter. Example: an Alaskan amber ale.

Munich Dunkel Lager: Rich, dark, and sweet, these beers also emphasize malt over hops. Big enough to stand up to a moderate level of spiciness from a rub or other technique, it should impart some caramel sweetness. Commercial example: A Mexican dark lager.

Sweet or Milk Stout: This uncommon style of stout has lactose or milk sugar added to it, which is un-fermentable by brewing yeast. This produces a rich and slightly sweet beer that is ideal for cooking, since it is low in bitterness. Packed with flavor, this beer can handle any bird, no matter how spicy. Commercial example: The classic was a stout from the UK, but I believe that beer is no longer made. Check with a craft brewery or brewpub for a local option.

Scottish or Scotch Ale: I use a Scottish Ale for my beer can chicken. Once again, it's a style of beer that emphasizes malt over hops, dark and rich, with a touch of smokiness that perfectly complements grilled foods.[v]

Gosh Thanks, Bill…It would have taken me 30 years to learn whatever you just said! What this tells me is that I'm not stuck with dumping a Cheap Beer, drinking a third of a good lager and pouring the rest into the Cheap Beer can.

Command formation

The rationale for this sub-title is that a headless chicken, standing up, with a beer can up its southern exposure, tends to look as if it's standing at attention. After you have selected your stout, ale, lager or wheat brew and situated the thoroughly rinsed and prepped fowl on the beer can (and likely the device that holds the beer can – two-thirds or so full of beer), take a moment to tend to two small details. But first – just because it's a *beer can*, which happens to be the right size for most dinner table chickens, doesn't mean the fluid in the can has to be beer. You might try a future hypothesis with white wine or cooking sherry, or something else – like variations on barbeque sauce, teriyaki, bourbon, a fizzy cola, fruit juices, and so on.

Boldly. Without parentheses – Detail one: wrap your little chicken drumstick terminals with tin foil booties – roughly one-third of the distance from the end of the leg to the joint with the thigh. This prevents the leg from over-cooking, even if you are using indirect grilling heat, which we will address presently.

Seasoning

Detail two: Before lighting the grill, apply your favorite rub to the *external* surfaces of the bird. Salts and peppers, chipotle seasoning, Italian or Latin, Asian or…make something up, and test it like a hypothesis.

Roasting

Make no mistake – this is roast chicken. Your outdoor oven – the grill – needs to get hot (300° - 350° F) but you won't want to place the bird directly over the fire. Depending on the size of your grill, you may find it necessary to build a tin foil dam around and under the chicken to catch dripping fat and juices, and to prevent flame-ups from scorching your dinner. With a five-burner grill, you should have enough room to get the entire contraption standing on the East side and two burners fired up to *medium* on the West side.

Fire in the hole: Light 'em up, close the lid, check every 15 minutes. All grills are different, so it may be necessary to adjust the heat and approximately one hour to hour and a half roasting time. Test for *done* with an oven-tested meat thermometer – to 165° F. Juices should run clear and joints should show no pink meat.

Serve with:

A Paul Simon CD, three to four friends and a pile of World Famous Potato Salad (the successful recipe for which is revealed in the NOBODY IS IMPORTANT chapter), and a summer ale. (April through August).

If you have two kids in high school, two home from college, and the neighbors detect (with envy) the music and aroma…it's impossibly easy to double the chicken. Your friends can double the beer.

Short version

Ingredients

Chicken – as many as your dinner party requires.

Beers – or other flavorful juices – in beer-can-size cans.

Spices – a rub for the outside of the bird (like cinnamon chipotle or a fowl-specific season salt. Season to taste).

Directions

Rinse the bird thoroughly in the kitchen sink.

If using a Beer Can Chicken Beer Can Holder – position holder(s) on the grill, then place a beer can ¾ full in the holder. Position the bird over the device and situate the legs to ensure the arrangement is stable. Wrap the end of the drumsticks with tin foil (about an inch to inch and a half).

Apply the spice rub or seasoning to the outside of the chicken.

Light the fire. Check periodically. If possible – roast over indirect heat. If using a small grill and indirect heat is not possible, it may be wise to place enough tin foil under the chicken and the beer can holder to prevent dripping juices from causing flare-ups.

Roast 1 to 1 ½ hours.

Serves: 4 humans per chicken.

Recipe for Success, with Indoctrination

Half of the punch-line for this parable is obvious – of course – and that's the discussion about helping your junior leaders move from wherever they were (grad school; another company; playing PS3 on mom's couch in the basement) through the membrane and into your organization. But it's deeper than that. It truly is a two-way yellow brick road. Not only do they need to learn your organization's processes, tools, language and culture, *they also bring their own unique knowledge and skills*, spices and flavors (for which you hired them).

That real-life opportunity to re-ionize as the oldest captain in the Marine Corps for three years could be interpreted as the Marine Corps, at war, seeking a bit more return on their initial investment: their ROI. The investment in my career by the Marine Corps, and ultimately by the tax-payer, was substantial. During those initial 22-plus years, I responded in kind. The Marine Corps and the taxpayer received more out of me than what they put in.

But after I retired, and after wandering through the private sector for 10 more years, the transition back through the membrane was not a perfectly fluid exercise. The whole experience had a Rip van Winkle character to it. Small and not-so-small changes in tactics and strategies, language, culture and technology soon gave me to understand that I had returned to an organization that was perpetually enduring yet continually evolving. Good thing I had avatars and mentors. I had some learnin' to do...

Your organization's "welcome aboard," orientation or indoctrination: Carefully select role models to lead your new team members through their first few months on the job. Use stories instead of PowerPoint to tell the organization's history and culture. Newer, more recently hired peers are a good choice for two reasons: peer-to-peer credibility and…the more recent hires will have a fresh appreciation for "What I <u>really</u> need to know during the first few weeks or months on the job." This can include: *where to park; the best places to eat; team/branch/division history, culture, successes and failures; how the performance appraisal process really works; how to get into the electronic time card on the intranet; company heroes; how to set up voice mail on the phone at the desk;* and on and on. Quiz 10 to 12 people who have been in your organization for fewer than 100 days and ask them: "What do you know now [about this organization] that you wish you knew three months ago?" Do the same with another crew at the six-month point.

The reason it is essential to task team members with about 100 days on the job is that they are still stinging from *not* having that essential information. Old hands – with years on the job – are well past the stage at which they just take it all for granted. *Everybody* knows where to park; *any* dummy can figure out voice mail. On the *however* side, <u>stories</u> from the Old Hands – about weathering past storms, leaping ethical hurdles and solving onerous problems – should complement the "what do I need to know during my first 100 days on the job?" indoc. Take a look at 6 months of trouble tickets and help desk calls: are people stuck on the same problems over and over? Why not catalog those common problems and teach the solutions as people walk in the door?

Through nearly 40 years, the most effective "orientation" I've experienced among the US Marine Corps, US Navy, Hughes Aircraft, Raytheon, Enron, and two other large private sector corporations…was the Marine Corps. Sure – we were learning "how to be Marines." Why can't we learn how to be Hughes, Enron or Raytheon consultants or entrepreneurs? I think the assumption is that most of the "how to" was supposed to have been learned in college, and the time spent in orientation is an overhead cost. These were all Fortune 500 corporations (or the equivalent). Overhead is a suck on profit. Orientation and training; teaching "how" for two to three months; is a *huge* suck on overhead. Sure – there's some middle ground between "three months of orientation" (boot camp) and "Hi! Welcome to Company X. Sign this W4. Sign this Non-Disclosure/Non-Compete Agreement. Sign these medical, dental and citizenship forms. Thank you…here's your desk…now get to work."

But – what's it worth to you?

What's missing in this is the "why?" (Social Psychology answers a lot of why senior leaders need to understand that "why.") Of the private sector companies I endured, one company's *Welcome* provided a professionally produced, week-long orientation, but completely devoid of organizational culture peculiar to their various business units around the country. Enron's two-day *Welcome,* on the other hand, offered not only more useful general information, in comparison, but also more of a sense for the organizational culture (innovation, for example). Still – it was only two days.

On your side of the osmosis chemistry – the bottom line goes back to my original essay and the example of The Container Store. Time spent in training and enculturation is an investment that pays royalties in company loyalty (lower turnover, less employee-driven loss, etc.) and higher profits.

What about the relationship between new employees and their new employers? A job posting on monster.com, careerbuilder.com, clearancejobs.com or sixfigurejobs.com will generally present a description of a given position along with the company's "resume:"

Company X is a recognized leader and global supplier in the design, manufacture and distribution of nature-friendly green stuff. We have 16,000 employees working in 43 countries, in happy, air-conditioned offices, surrounded by lots of green trees and green plants. We have competitive salaries and the best environmentally friendly benefits in our industry, including matching 100 percent of the first five percent of employee 401(k) contributions. (and so on...)(lots of companies do something like this.)

In parallel, prospects submit their resumes, tell their stories (just like the hiring companies do on their web sites) and hope for interviews. At the interview, prospect and hiring company are literally peers, both seeking a transaction. Either one can walk away. So why – when Junior Leader Joes or Junior Leader Jennifers receive (and accept) job offers, are they all of a sudden treated like company idiots? Why – if your organization is paying $60,000 to $100,000 a year to hire really brilliant people with kick-ass resumes – would you then pay $2000 to $5000 a day for a "consultant?" Your new junior leaders *are* your consultants!

Why does this happen (and still happen a lot)? Based on experience and observation, it's a matter of Knowledge Management. At the heyday of the "dot.com" boom...at the start of this concept of Knowledge Management, organizations around the globe made seats at the table for the

CKO: the Chief Knowledge Officer. Much of the knowledge they collected, stored and made available for their corporate peers was focused on ISO 9000 and Six Sigma processes. Too few organizations sought to catalogue the wealth of knowledge resident in their own employees. They still don't. Most of these organizations have little more depth of information about their own people than 3 mils – the thickness of a resume, but terabytes of rules, policies and ISO 9000 processes.

The Armed Forces today are still working on how to provide decision-makers with easily and rapidly accessible, usable information on things like how many Urdu and Pashto speakers we have in uniform; who knows how to run a desalination plant or citywide electrical grid (in the wake of an earthquake in someplace like Haiti); and where to find the Reservists who know something about assisting with elections (for countries with shaky, emerging democracies). This is why those two sergeants don't re-enlist: the fellow who speaks Korean is assigned to Panama while the guy who speaks native Spanish gets orders to Korea. And in your organization – you may have a new hire who writes video game software in ToonBoom, Cold Fusion, Visual Basic and C++ as a hobby…cleaning toilets and checking IDs.

Your organization needs a simple, logical way to catalog and access the problem-solving skills of your incoming team members. If those thousands of resumes are stuck in the "shared folders" of the HR department and in the mental thumb drive of the manager who hired them – it's no wonder some of your team members start feeling irrelevant by the time they have logged 6 months to a year on the job, if not much sooner. The questions, simply, are: what else do you know…or know how to do…other than what we hired you for?

What all of *this* boils down to is: Your organizational knowledge is the beer in the can, absorbed from within. That spice rub on the outside comes with a lot of different ingredients and represents the influence from the outside world of business: competitors, customers, stock holders, the environment. The relationship between your new junior leaders and your organization *must* be a two-way Yellow Brick Road. The spices, flavors, ingredients and new ideas coming into your team from the inside and the outside, through organizational osmosis, are potentially the ROI – Return on *Indoctrination*

And so – back to the concept that your ideal leaders are theories. You won't know until you test your hypotheses.

Marine Corps Leadership Principles

Keep your people informed. Know your people.
Employ your team in accordance with its capabilities.

Vol. 3 No. 6 **FOCUS** June 2007

Just one enemy: *outside* the wire

First – an update is appropriate. In our last exciting adventure, I was zipping up the FOCUS Newsletter in preparation for a deployment to Iraq, beginning in August 2006. I had hoped to continue writing – updating my web site, and the newsletter in particular, in the few minutes a week we had access to e-mail (because I was expecting to return to my civilian occupation following my trip to the *Sandbox*). Once deployed to Camp Fallujah, al-Anbar Province, I discovered I did not have access to my web site. From a business standpoint, this was marginally acceptable, as I was not doing *executive coaching* or running Leadership seminars while deployed anyway.

Following the deployment to Iraq, I returned to my "day job" in the Marine Corps and resumed teaching graduate students, part time in the evenings, with George Washington University – in Consulting Skills and Organizational Diagnosis. In combination with the seven-month assignment in Iraq, these courses with GWU continued to provide my journal with stories, metaphors and case studies for practical application to Leadership and Conflict Management. (Seven months in Iraq...conflict management – get it?) But it was no joke, and my assignment focused on the analysis of internal conflicts in Iraqi politics, religious extremists, terrorist financing and economic reconstruction in Anbar Province.

One of the easy lessons from this is that the conflict in Iraq, as a whole, is a case study in dysfunctional organizations. Iraq's central government is hosed up and the Sunni majority in Anbar Province still doesn't trust the Shi'ite majority government.* The easiest take-away from seven months in the *Sandbox* is the realization that <u>internal</u> conflicts are likely the biggest detractor to accomplishing a mission – within not only the Iraqi central government, but in America's armed forces, the U.S. federal government and the private sector as well. This is one of those *Nero fiddles while Rome burns* stories. The lesson for leaders in Corporate America is to figure out who your real adversaries are…to train your team members to do the same. Internal conflict between two employees (or between two departments) on the same team detracts from your mission. If you are in business to make a profit, time spent on internal conflict is time NOT focused on your customer or real mission…the people who write your paychecks and keep your lights on. Two employees fighting over a parking spot are fighting over a parking spot and not selling your over-priced jeans and T-shirts.

Conflicts are inevitable…now what?

Camp Fallujah is a *forward operating base,* or FOB. The FOB is enclosed in a 10-foot-high concrete block wall with razor wire strung along the 8-mile perimeter. The bad guys are outside the wire. The good guys are on my side of the wire – until they go on patrols. It's easy in Iraq to tell the difference between a petty argument (Hey! Who took the last cup of coffee and didn't make a fresh pot?!) and a disagreement with life-or-death consequences. The bad guys may be on the other side of the wire, but they have mortars and rockets, some with a range of at least 10 miles. They use them. This is one of those disagreements we have with them. When they shoot at us, we shoot back. During my 189 days in the combat zone, the bad guys outside the wire lobbed occasional rockets and mortars into Camp Fallujah a couple of times a week. We responded in kind.

In sharp contrast, the first week I was home from the *Sandbox*, in Dallas, TX, I was invited to sit in on a homeowner association meeting, with friends – but not in my own neighborhood. I was a guest but I had a different interest in the subdivision (I had flown in to Dallas to re-connect with my daughter after my deployment). It was the annual meeting to elect new board members and take up other business. Aside from voting on new board members, homeowner associations can face some ugly issues: "Your dog pooped in my flowerbed." and "My neighbors party late… and loud." and "The guy on the corner mows his lawn at 6 a.m. every Saturday!" (Genuine combat, just like Anbar Province.)

In this case, the issue was whether or not to lawfully evict a neighbor who had moved into the neighborhood when the subdivision was new. He owned an expensive motor home, and parked his motor home in his driveway on a regular basis. He said the sales representative told him it was acceptable – as long as it was not visible from the street. (He kept it out of sight behind a gate and trees in large planters with casters that rolled into place to further hide the motor home. The motor home truly was not visible from the street.) Most of his neighbors apparently wanted him to get rid of the vehicle – to park the motor home at a storage facility specifically because he was violating the original deed restrictions. In Texas, the "homeowner association by-laws" are typically boilerplate, and written by professional homeowner association management companies. This set of by-laws restricted recreational vehicles from being parked on, at, near or behind these $500,000-to-$600,000 homes for more than 96 hours. In other words – restricted to when someone else visits for three or four days. Stow your own motor home in a paid storage facility. He refused. He asked for new by-laws.

At first blush, it may seem there are three easy answers to this dilemma: Modify the rules and allow the fellow (your neighbor inside the wire) to keep his motor home parked, out of sight, alongside his house. Or – forget about it and leave the guy alone. Or – the motor home owner could realize *he* is the source of the problem and just bend to the wishes of the majority and the association by-laws. (Make a new pot of coffee when you drain it.)

Afforded the opportunity to make these observations to the assembled homeowner association, I pointed out that this neighbor was "inside the wire." He did not represent the kind of external threat to the subdivision that they *could have* been focused on, like sex offenders, drug dealers, taxes, burglars, tornados and hurricanes. I also suggested that if this fellow and his wife could afford a $600,000 home and a $250,000 motor home – they likely could afford $100/month to store it off site. The homeowner association found the "conflict management" reference amusing, but declined to amend their by-laws.

It's often easy to see a solution when it's someone else's problem. Neither side in this case would back down. War is a clash of wills, a clash of motivations. Both sides were ready to go to war over principle. The question is: Whom do you include on your side of the wire? Of course people have issues, and their issues are important to them, at the time. Conflict is inevitable…but it helps to put things in perspective.

Oh…and the unbendable guy moved his motor home to storage. He and his wife also sold their house and moved on – to what they hoped would be a friendlier community.

* (US troops are now out of Iraq and in 2013, turmoil and uncertainty remain.)

Recipe for Success, with Cabbage Rolls

...and Dirty Bread

Cabbage Rolls are a complete meal, with carbs, protein, veggies and a little fat. Or more fat – like the grilled stuffed pepper recipe in a later chapter. To totally balance this Hungarian-inspired fare and acknowledge the Hungarian-American foundations running through New York, New Jersey, Pennsylvania, Ohio and Michigan, ice down a case of traditional amber lager from Pennsylvania and crank up some Bruce Springsteen.

(No – The Boss is not of Hungarian extraction. But his music *ROCKS the USA!* Ex-relatives of the author hail from the Hungarian-American stock that settled in Ohio. Now concentrate. Get back to the recipe...)

<u>Ingredients</u>

Dirty Bread

Fatback: (Hungarian: *szalonna*, for bacon.) You can find this delicacy at a butcher shop – smoked or uncured, or as packaged "salt pork" in the bacon section of your local grocery store. For a family reunion, you will need three to four ½ pound blocks. Fatback takes center stage in a range of ethnic recipes, from Poland and Russia, France and Mexico, or US Southern cooking with collard greens. Today – it's Hungarian.

Bread: For this – no soft commercial bread (loaded with high-fructose corn syrup) will do. Depending on where you live and the talents of your local boulangerie, you can use a couple of loaves of Italian, Cuban or French bread.

Wash, peel and slice three to four cucumbers into thin slices. (Use a potato peeler to peel off long, thin slices.)

1 baseball-size sweet onion, diced.

2-3 bell peppers: Green is fine, but a mix of red, yellow or orange with green bell pepper adds color to the meal. Diced.

2-3 fresh tomatoes: Two to three diced, ripe beefsteak tomatoes. Hothouse or ugly tomatoes are just as good, or cherry tomatoes – halved.

Spices: Salt and pepper are the standards. You may find a use for a dash of garlic salt, or steak seasoning. Creole seasonings are excellent on almost everything. I wouldn't try soy or teriyaki; I might consider hot or sweet paprika, or chipotle or other Tex-Mex flavors.

Cabbage Rolls

Cabbage: Start with a fresh head. You may need two. If you try "standard" green cabbage on your first hypothesis, try Napa cabbage the next time – it can be a bit more flexible. Remove the external, unusable leaves. Each portion of the completed recipe will require 2-3 leaves (depending on the appetites around your backyard picnic table). Cut off the bottoms of the cabbage and separate 12-15 leaves. Prepare a kettle of water for boiling. Dunk the cabbage leaves in boiling water. Don't over-cook. (One minute may be more than adequate.)

Meat

Standard (and always yummy) is ground beef. Brown one pound for approximately 6-8 leaves. Two pounds for a larger table.

Alternatives: Ground turkey (much lower fat – can compensate for the bacon fat you're fixin' to drip on the dirty bread). Or – Shrimp: If pre-cooked, cut into ½ inch chunks.

1 cup cooked white rice.

1 onion, diced

2 eggs

Garlic salt and coarse ground pepper to taste

Directions

If this is an almost genuine Hungarianesque back-yard family reunion cook-out, prepare a 3-foot circle of five-pound boulders in the southwest corner of your back yard, filled with seasoned oak or hickory firewood or four 10-pound bags of charcoal. If this proves impractical, one of those inexpensive charcoal grills, with a grate and a lid, will work fine – with a lot less charcoal. Get the charcoal a-blaze, and when half of the coals are gray around the edges:

Bread: Slice the loaves longitudinally (not Texas toast bread "steaks") in chunks of about 4 to 6 inches each and place these close enough to the fire to apply dripping fatback.

Veggies: Position the chopped, sliced veggies in bowls or trays near the bread.

Szalonna / bacon / fatback: Sharpen the end of a ½-inch diameter stick and poke this through a block of fatback (through the rind). A stick with a forked end works even better. With a sharp knife, make cuts on the block of fatback on the side opposite the rind. Hold the fatback over the fire and rotate until the fat starts dripping. Shift position to aim that dripping fat onto the bread. Continue this ritual while listening to The Boss (either your wife or Bruce Springsteen), drinking an amber lager and telling lies with your cousins, uncles and next-door neighbors.

As you season sections of bread with fatback drippings, call the family over to grab a hunk of bread, layer with the slices of cucumbers, onions, peppers and tomatoes, and some more drippings. (Cut off small pieces of crisp fatback to add as another topping.)

Cabbage Rolls

Boil the cabbage leaves a minute or less – to soften, then drain and set them aside on a baking dish or dinner plate.

Brown the ground beef or ground turkey, or apply the cut shrimp morsels. For an interesting flavor, heat a large skillet with 2 tbsp olive oil and 2 tbsp soy sauce; brown the beef or turkey. Drain. Add the rice, onion, eggs, and seasoning. If using pre-cooked shrimp – add these last and mix completely. (If starting with uncooked shrimp, boil first in a separate kettle. Shrimp are done when they are pink and form a letter "C." Don't over-cook as they will return to the grill with the cooked rice and other ingredients.)

Spoon the meat/onion/rice filling on to a cabbage leaf and roll to form a log – about 2 ½ inches long and 1 ½ inch in diameter. Secure with a toothpick.

Place all completed cabbage rolls on tin foil and place on a grill heated to approx. 300-350° F for 30-45 minutes.

Serve with:

Springsteen: *Live / 1975-85*, Traditional lager, and seven of your closest friends.

Short version

<u>Ingredients</u>

Fat-back (Szalonna, or salt pork), 2 – 3 ½ lb packages

Bread – 1 or 2 loaves French, Cuban or Italian, sliced in half, length-wise

Cucumbers – 2-3 large, peeled cukes, for slices, also length-wise

Tomatoes – 2-3, sliced or diced, or cherry tomatoes, halved

Onion – ½ sliced or diced (dice the other ½ for the Cabbage Rolls)

Bell pepper – 2, sliced or diced

Cabbage – green or Napa, 2 heads

Ground beef – 1 to 2 lbs (depending on the size of your audience)

Rice – white, brown or wild rice (or mixed); 1 cup dry rice before cooking

1 tsp Garlic salt

1 tsp Coarse-ground black pepper

2 Eggs

<u>Directions</u>

Cabbage Rolls

Cut the bottoms off the cabbage. Remove the external leaves and collect the next 8-10 large, usable leaves. You might chose to submerge the leaves in boiling water briefly to soften them. Don't over-cook.

Brown the ground beef (or other choice). Add the rice, onion, eggs, and seasoning. If using pre-cooked shrimp – add these last and mix completely

Spoon the meat/onion/rice filling on to a cabbage leaf and roll to form a log – about 2 ½ inches long and 1 ½ inch in diameter. Secure with a toothpick.

Place all completed cabbage rolls on tin foil and place on a grill heated to approx. 300° - 350°F for 30-45 minutes.

Dirty Bread

While waiting for the Cabbage Rolls...

With a commercial vegetable wash product, or ½ cup grapefruit juice in a large mixing bowl filled with water – clean (de-wax) the cucumbers, tomatoes and bell peppers. Slice or dice these and the onion (reserve ½ of the onion for the cabbage rolls)

Score the fat side of the salt pork; mount on the end of a sharp stick (or long "marshmallow and weenie roaster fork.") through the rind side. Hold the salt pork over a hot charcoal fire and rotate until the fat starts dripping. Drip the fat onto the sliced bread. Once seasoned (but not saturated), call guests to tear off individual servings of bread, top with vegetables and onion, and some additional fat-back drippin's.

Recipe for Success, with Solutions & Suspensions

While *The enemy outside the wire* may read like yet another chapter in conflict management, the essay is really about judgment and decisiveness; solutions and suspensions. It's about picking your battles.

Fighting cholesterol and the battle of your waist line requires good judgment and conscious decisions too, but you can be selective on what you stuff those cabbage rolls with (minced shrimp, chopped turkey breast or tofu (light tofu) or – diced porterhouse or top end ground beef); you could substitute olive oil, canola, or safflower oil for bacon fat on that dirty bread and clean it up some. Or – you could strive for balance over the course of a week…have the dirty bread with fatback drippings on Saturday and switch to corn flakes with skim milk (and leafy green vegetables on the side) for the next six days.

Or not.

Congress' mid-summer 2011 battles over debt and deficit sought to achieve balance – between social liberals and fiscal conservatives. As of late July, both sides had picked their battles and as August 2nd loomed no compromise appeared imminent. Like the neighbor with the motor home, this became a manufactured threat while our nation had external threats that should have been commanding more attention. Sadly, the result of this internecine Congressional conflict wiped out more wealth than the initial recession following 9/11 in 2001 – more damage than was caused by terrorists on 9/11.[vi] [vii] All of this was due to an unwillingness to compromise.

When it comes to dirty bread, there is no real compromise on fat. Olive oil has a place in the cave and in the Grilling Studio – and dirty bread isn't dirty bread with olive oil. This is a time for bacon grease (not congressional pork). So the question devolves to "How do we find a solution?"

Remember that 10th grade science demonstration where the science teacher puts a couple of two-liter beakers on the work table, with the black table tops, at the front of the class… and pours half a cup of table salt into one beaker full of water and half a cup of flour or dirt in the other – also full of water? Student volunteers stir the contents of the two containers for two minutes or so and the class takes notes on what they see. The next day – after the two containers have been left to settle to an undisturbed state, the students make further observations and record their notes. The salt appears to have dissolved in the water, creating a solution (similar to (but obviously not exactly the same as) the saline solution used by people who wear contact lenses). The saline solution is clear, transparent and allows light to pass through.

The flour (or dirt) mixture is cloudy on the first day, slightly less so on the second. The flour or dirt particles have not been absorbed or dissolved, but instead are *suspended* in the water. Because the flour or dirt particles will not break down to ion size (like the sodium chloride / salt) and mix with the ions of water (hydrogen and oxygen) they will remain suspended until all of the particles eventually fall to the bottom of the column of water.

There is a parallel with the US military presence in Iraq and Afghanistan. Absent the clarity of knowledge that comes with understanding other cultures, we can be either *Suspended* in a murky situation (as the mixture is constantly stirred by combat) or a *Solution*. As the adage goes: If you're not part of the solution, you're part of the problem. History will tell. (Many in the conventional US Armed Forces do not do well with understanding other cultures. Special Operations operators, on the other hand, are keenly aware of this need.) The lack of genuine understanding of other cultures, early on, prevented the US-led coalition from delivering real solutions in either Iraq or Afghanistan.

How this translates to your organization: In many organizations, the front-line manager (leader) may be the most-junior of the salaried employees in the company. Those who are supervised may range from newly hired hourly employees to veteran hourly employees (who may actually earn more on an annual basis than the so-called front-line manager. These are like 2nd and 1st lieutenants in the Marine Corps or Army.). Those senior to the front-line manager represent both the old guard who may have started the company and the intermediate and senior leaders in engineering, production, distribution, sales, human resources or whatever your organization's divisions.

The greatest challenge for front-line managers (including lieutenants) might be those hourly employees who are new-hires. In some industries, turnover is 100% per year or more. Those new employees are *suspended* in the organization. Keeping an eye on both their performance and their acculturation: do they become ionized and accept the profit-making processes (missions) of the corporation, or...do they muddy the waters until they eventually sink to the bottom? Front-line managers (your junior leaders) deal with a range of problem-solving dilemmas on a daily basis.

Recommendation: Coaching junior leaders in the Arcanum of solving other people's problems, have them bring the adversaries together to state their disagreements, then state their proposed solutions, *then* explain how their proposed solutions contribute to superior quality products or services, increased market share or increased revenue. If none of their disagreements and solutions improve the organization's products or service, or positively impact profitability, they must be <u>distractions</u> that reduce productivity. In other words, if we're fighting over whether to mow the lawn with a red lawn mower or a blue lawn mower – we're fighting, not mowing. Tell them to take it out back after work, solve their own issues, and get back to the bottom line.[viii]

This is the bottom line.

Marine Corps Leadership Trait:
Judgment

Marine Corps Leadership Principle:
Make Sound and Timely Decisions

Vol. 1 No. 5 **FOCUS** May 2005

A butterfly was spotted crossing the street

No metaphors in this chapter. This chapter clearly addresses Ambiguity, Uncertainty and Disorder.

Leaders deal with ambiguity all the time. The sentence: A *Butterfly was spotted crossing the street*, is ambiguous precisely because I wrote it in the *passive voice*. Flash back to high school English Composition class: When you write a sentence in the *active voice* (like the one you're reading), you tell the reader who the actor is. You clarify who is responsible for the action. Ambiguity dissolves. I wrote that sentence. Subject-Verb-Object clarity.

Ambiguity can lead to chaos (in the pedestrian sense of chaos): Two drivers reach intersecting stop signs at the north and west corners of an intersection at apparently the same moment. Forget 'driver's ed....' There is some statistical probability that two drivers will *both* accelerate at the same moment. We don't know the probability for *these* two drivers, but Americans have been killing each other with cars, with predictable regularity, to the tune of about 40,000 KIA *each* year for decades (about ¾ of all American losses in 11 years of war in Vietnam – every year for 50 years. The annual total hasn't been less than 30,000 since World War II.). We know, driving to work each day, that disaster will strike somewhere

– that someone dies on America's roads once every 15 minutes. We just don't, in advance, know who.

That's just the problem with uncertainty – we can be certain it will strike, but we cannot be certain where. Like the weather, we can model it, but our prediction of *where* it will strike is imperfect.

That *certain uncertainty* is no trick. In fact, *certain uncertainty* bears a remarkable similarity to the formal study of CHAOS. Mathematicians and computer programmers dislike the idea of applying Chaos Theory to studies in sociology, psychology or ethics. Chaos Theory should be used to predict the weather and other apparently chaotic, random events – but which have underlying causes and observable effects – not to predict human behavior:

"The two main components of chaos theory are the ideas that systems – no matter how complex they may be – rely upon an underlying order, and that very simple or small systems and events can cause very complex behaviors or events. This latter idea is known as *sensitive dependence on initial conditions*, a circumstance discovered by Edward Lorenz.

"The *butterfly effect*, first described by Lorenz at the December 1972 meeting of the American Association for the Advancement of Science in Washington, D.C., vividly illustrates the essential idea of chaos theory...."Predictability: Does the Flap of a Butterfly's Wings in Brazil set off a Tornado in Texas?" The example of such a small system as a butterfly being responsible for creating such a large and distant system as a tornado in Texas illustrates the impossibility of making predictions for complex systems; despite the fact that these are determined by underlying conditions, precisely what those conditions are can never be sufficiently articulated to allow long-range predictions."[ix]

In a practical sense, what this means is that when the weather service predicts a 70 percent chance of rain, we can be fairly certain that 70 percent of an area will get wet, but we cannot be certain where those raindrops will fall. (The idea that my home has a 7 in 10 chance of rain is not accurate.) The chaos of one thundershower is rather like the chaos of another thundershower. Never identical, just similar enough to give it the name *thundershower*. Predictable unpredictability. Tow truck drivers can be certain there will be 22 traffic accidents in metro Houston, TX, on a given rush hour morning, Monday through Friday, year after year – but not certain where. Fern branches, snowflakes, coast lines and (perhaps) even stock markets exhibit this predictable unpredictability.

This is *exactly* where the overlap with human behavior comes into play. Those traffic accidents all have common causes: excessive speed, failure to maintain a safe distance at a given speed, impatience, distractions (like cell phones and texting), and yes…ambiguity. *Individual* human behavior is not something we can graph or predict with mathematical precision. Yet in the aggregate, over time, human behavior in a given setting is not only comprehensible but predictable. Categories of causes of traffic accidents are the same from country to country, city to city, day after day, over and over and over. The causes of *chaos in business are* common from one company to the next, day after day. Lack of communication; lack of vision; lack of focus; morale problems; uncertainty; lay-offs; and so on. These are your butterflies. Lorenz and his cohort of really smart people refer to these change agents as "strange attractors."

In our "No Monopoly on Leadership" game, seminar participants each take a role to play – the *opposite* of one of the 14 Marine Corps Leadership Traits: Dependability, Bearing, Courage, Decisiveness, Endurance, Enthusiasm, Tact, Initiative, Integrity, Judgment, Justice, Knowledge, Unselfishness and Loyalty. The player with the *integrity* card plays the game dishonestly; the *courage* card plays timidly; the *knowledge* card plays with ignorance, and so on. The result for a simple board game? Chaos. The results in corporate America? Chaos.

Finally, we bring this into the workplace: Return to Lorenz' concept of *sensitive dependence on initial conditions*. Your corporate culture is the "initial condition" your team members plug in to every day. Change one thing, one strange attractor – a grumpy manager, news of a takeover bid, budget cuts, a flaring ego, a single rumor about layoffs or outsourcing, and we have introduced uncertainty. Ambiguity. Without leadership, the spiraling chaos leads directly from uncertainty and ambiguity through morale, quality, safety, efficiency and productivity to profitability.

Spotted or striped – find the butterfly.

Kill it.

Recipe for Success, with Shish Kebab

<u>Prep Time</u>: 30 Minutes; 40 Minutes with sausage

Cook Time: about 10 minutes

Ready in: an hour

Servings: 12

Tunes: Guitar riff: Mason Williams – Classical Gas, or Dire Straits: Sultans of Swing

Brew: a bottled beer from the Philippines or Japan.

<u>Ingredients</u>

1 pound (approx.) lean beef. London broil steak, trimmed

1 pound shrimp, peeled, de-veined

1 pound chicken breast, skinless, boneless

1 pound sausage – beer brats or Italian sausage

1 fresh (or two cans) cubed pineapple

1 quart cherry or grape tomatoes, rinsed

2 green peppers

½ pound shallots, peeled, cubed

1 quart fresh button mushrooms, w/o stems, rinsed (halved, quartered or whole, depending on size)

30-40 bamboo skewers

Teriyaki marinade

Directions

Place bamboo skewers in a 9-inch baking dish. Place a second, smaller baking dish on top of the skewers (to keep the skewers submerged), then add water to the bottom pan to pre-soak skewers – so they won't ignite on the grill. Soak at least 20 minutes.

Cut sausage into 1-inch sections. With cooking spray or 1 tsp olive oil, start sausage browning in a skillet on low temp. Turn frequently.

Cube beef and chicken. Place in individual bowls with teriyaki marinade. If using pre-cooked shrimp – peel and remove tails. Place in individual bowl with teriyaki marinade.

Check on the sausage.

Clean, rinse, wash, slice and cube pineapple, tomatoes, peppers, shallots and mushrooms. Goal: bite-size pieces that fit on a stick.

Check on the sausage.

ASSEMBLE THE SKEWERS! BUILD THE KEBABS! FIRE UP THE GRILL! GET ANOTHER BEER! CHANGE THE MUSIC!!! CALL IN THE MARINES!

With a mission-impossible-quality team of friends and neighbors – all certified to be able to walk with scissors – you can be reasonably certain that most of them can handle cherry tomatoes, morsels of raw chicken and bamboo sticks with pencil-pointy ends. Maintain situational awareness.

Position the meats, veggies and fruits on the skewers. Seek assistance from friends and neighbors.

Some grill masters like to assemble the ingredients so that all skewers are relatively uniform in appearance. Some like to keep their shrimp-on-sticks and tomatoes-on-sticks separate and place them over the embers near the end of the cycle. Those who smash all of the ingredients together haphazardly may claim that the overlapping flavors – from pineapple to shrimp, shallots to beef – make the event. However you do it…the tomatoes (and mushrooms) and shrimp are likely your lowest common denominator and need the least time over the fire. Three to five minutes is the limit, depending on how hot the grill is. With this hypothesis – depending on your grill and attention to detail – rotate the chicken and beef skewers at 2-3 minutes on high heat. If the shrimp are pre-cooked, 2-3 minutes on a lower heat may be adequate. Maintain situational awareness.

Fini. Serve.

If dining near the grill – shut down the grill and close the lid between servings. Leave the next skewers to remain warm on the grill…for seconds and thirds.

Enjoy.

Getting to the Point, with Situational Awareness

Sometimes it helps to stop talking, stop telling stories, and…start paying attention:

So I'm walking through an airport terminal, having moments before gained the respect and admiration of the TSA employees in their dark blue shirts (which 70 years ago in another country would have been Brown Shirts), as I had removed my glasses, wallet, foil-wrapped gum, shoes, dynamite-laden leather belt with a 17-inch long samurai blade hidden in the buckle, the nitro-glycerin infused cell phone, calcium-ammonium nitrate injected winter jacket, secret agent decoder wedding ring and the most recent edition of a local newspaper bemoaning the most recent string of losses by the professional neighborhood hockey, football or basketball team…from my person, and correctly placed my sock-footed feet on the yellow footprints… (Placing my feet on the yellow footprints always brings back fond memories of Marine Corps boot camp.)…when I came upon and instantly recognized a fellow traveler, from my home office, returning to the metropolitan community I was in the process of exiting, whereupon I could apply various legal syntactic and grammatical devices, such as opening and closing parens, commas, semicolons, adjuncts, apostrophes and apologies to extend this introduction by many paragraphs and so draw attention to the lack of brevity in my discourse, akin to Herman Melville's sentence from *Moby Dick* – exceeding 100 words – about whales and other cetaceous creatures from Melville's ponderous imagination, but as my intent is not to draw attention to either my avoidance of brevity (I'm in the process these days of reading Charles Dickens' *Great Expectations* (on my Droid), with its own peculiarly long, ambling, first person narratives...or myself, I would be inclined to comment that my colleague – chance-met in Airside Terminal A – and I are both engaged in the regular "day job" of disrupting the lives of terrorists, and therefore both steeped in the formal and informal lore of *operational security*, more casually known in our circles as *OPSEC*. One of the elements of OPSEC is maintaining a low profile...becoming a *hard target* and not a *soft target* for the bad guys. It was therefore singularly amusing that this fellow should present himself coursing through Airside Terminal A as the spectre of a renowned professional wrestler...with a T shirt (and pects, lats, traps and biceps) and ball cap signifying his allegiance to a particular brand of Special Operations. (Low profile?)

But the chance meeting with "Bill" gave me pause to consider my own low profile. When I travel, commercially, I like to relax. And so, having left the office where we concoct plots to disrupt the machinations of various terrorist tribes, I stopped in the men's room to change out of my $90 dress trousers and $150 dress shoes and into $89 jeans and $149 cowboy boots. With my Vietnam-era ball cap with embroidered patches that identified me as a pensioner with enduring ties to our nation's armed forces.

Low profile? Bill and I were both targets. Hard to pay attention when you're not paying attention...It's hard to listen to your customer while you're telling stories.

A Rubik's Cube of Rubik's Cubes

What's the point, especially in the private sector? The world – the whole world – has become such an amazingly complex operating environment for even small businesses that the entrepreneur absolutely has to maintain an awareness of politics in China, fuel subsidies in Nigeria, the weather's impact on agriculture in Florida, Peru and Vietnam, religious extremism in the Middle East, presidential politics in the United States and Russia, nuclear ambitions in Iran and North Korea (and the impact on oil prices (and that impact on delivery prices for American commodities (and that impact on commodity prices (and that impact on wages...), not to mention slacker nations like Portugal, Italy, Ireland, Spain and Greece (and their impact on the US stock market and global prices of gold or oil), corruption in numerous countries across Africa, narco-terrorism in Mexico, the release of the next 4G or 5G nano phone, coal in West Virginia, healthcare legislation, operating our businesses in the cloud, China's rise and some other country's fall, and personal (as well as business) identity security) and...)))))). These *all* impact business. Every business.

Some people thrive on the thrill of complexity in a fast-paced environment. Some do not.

I think about it like this: In the 1920s, business in one market – manufacturing cars, for example – was like one face of a Rubik's Cube. In the 1960's – more like a complete Rubik's Cube. Now, in 2012 – it's more like a Rubik's Cube of Rubik's Cubes. A Rubik's cube (which I have never solved once undone) has 27 blocks (- nominally. Discount the multi-dimensional axles, including the one in the center.), and each block (a cube) has six sides, for a total of 162 faces. If we imagine a Rubik's Cube of Rubik's cubes, 27 cubed is 19,683 blocks and 162 faces cubed is 4,251,528.

Are there really four and a quarter million faces on 27X27X27 Rubik's Cubes? Yes. Are there four and a quarter million issues to deal with on every problem? Is life really that complex?

Well...yes. Sort of. And it's evolving exponentially faster every year. But most of us blank out the distractions we can't deal with. Example: In the US, about 450 movies (roughly two hours each) were released in each recent year back through at least 2005. That's about 900 hours of viewing time each year. (If you've watched them all, every year – you might be unemployed. You're only awake about 5700 hours each year and you might be working about 2900 of those hours.) Television is on 24 hours a day, and in my market, there are hundreds and hundreds of channels. We have dozens of radio stations, and the local bookstore racks *display* hundreds of magazines, not to mention tens of thousands of book titles in scores of genres. The on-line sources offer zillions more. And then there's Facebook, Twitter, Linked-In, YouTube, e-mail at work and home, text messages and...the telephone. Don't forget the occasional trip to professional (or semi-pro) baseball, hockey, basketball or football games. Or your own kids' games. Even your own marathons, ultras and triathlons. Oh yeah – and work. Don't forget the information load at *work*.

The point? We're selective in what we attend to.

Checking on the sausage is Situational Awareness. The domains of neuroscience and cognitive psychology offer far more detail about human ability to "pay attention to" more than one thing at a time than we can discuss in an allegorical recipe, but what we can teach our junior leaders is OPSEC.

Operational Security – OPSEC – in commerce is all about paying attention, being aware, and prioritizing stimuli. We can't tell from the sound of sausage cooking if it's done enough to skewer. We can't tell by the smell – until it's overdone. We can't really tell by taste – although after 3-4 minutes of simmering it probably smells really yummy. After a few minutes, the outside is already hot, but absent a meat thermometer test on a statistically valid sample of sausage bits (a bit over the top for shish kebab) we can't be absolutely certain the core is done enough to probe with bamboo sticks – by touch. And we can't visually inspect the insides without ruining the sausage bit. Much of this is based on experience. When we teach junior leaders – we need to replicate experience…

Yes – we're grilling, but what *this* boils down to is RISK. In the military world of OPSEC, it's all about reducing risk to our troops. We want them to learn how to maintain a low profile, especially when working or traveling overseas – in order to reduce risk. In commerce – take manufacturing for example – risk can be measured in terms of Risk to Personnel, Risk to Capital Equipment, Risk to a Business Segment's Ability to Generate Revenue, and Risk to the Environment. (The ability to generate revenue may be impacted by factors that may or may not threaten capital equipment – like extended blizzards, hurricanes or poor maintenance standards.)

The overlapping narrative for any of these domains – military, government, private sector, non-profit or education – is *Risk to Personnel*. Those people are little sausages, and if your junior leaders are not aware of their situations, if they don't check on them frequently, your team will spoil the environment, will destroy capital equipment and will deplete your ability to generate revenue uninterrupted. Our little Soldiers and Marines will lapse into faulty habits, and we want to take care of them because we care.

Our team members don't come to work with neon signs on their foreheads that announce: "I had an argument with my wife," or "I have a gambling, drug or alcohol problem," or "One of my parents has Alzheimer's or cancer," or "I suffer from depression," or "I'm having problems with my teenager," or "I just found out *I* have cancer," or "I can't pay my bills and the phone calls from creditors are on my mind while I'm on the $60,000 lathe."

Stop talking. Pay attention. Get to the point. Prioritize.

As for butterflies and ambiguity – uncertainty is a recipe for risk.

Marine Corps Leadership Principle

Know your team and look out for their welfare.

Vol. 2 No. 6 **FOCUS** June 2006

Change is Imperative; Change is Impossible

After I retired from the Marine Corps (the first time) in 1995, I served as a training manager at General Motors in Detroit (as a contractor through subsidiary Hughes Aircraft); then in business development and training management with Raytheon at NASA's Johnson Space Center; and finally as a training manager at Enron. For me, Enron was a short roller coaster – straight to the top of the pay scales for a training manager, and straight to the bottom rungs of self-employment, 18 months later.

In a sense, that experience of being one of the first laid off from Enron in early December 2001 could be the ideal metaphor for Change Management. But what a change. Like others in my middle-age age group, I was painfully aware that one rarely accumulates personal wealth working for someone else. I knew colleagues bringing in $200,000 to $400,000 a year as independent consultants. We would have lunch or go out for a beer, and I would say, "That's what I'm gonna be when I grow up."

The test had come when I approached one of these independents, on contract to teach 6 Sigma seminars at Raytheon (not long before I moved from Raytheon to Enron), and asked him to bring me into his private consulting practice. I knew I could do what he was doing, if only he'd carve off a piece of the work and let me get started. His reply: "I don't make money finding work for guys like you. If I throw you a bone, and you succeed, who's going to find you the next one? Me? I don't think so. Quit your job, and when you can make it on your own [find your own contracts] for a year, come back and see me – I'd be more than happy to work *with* you."

Quit my job? Impossible! My military pension wasn't enough to live on; it wasn't even enough to make my monthly mortgage payment. Then there was the wife and (then-) infant child, the two car payments, cable TV, telephone, utilities, keeping my beer cooler stocked, fire ant killer, fishing tackle, golf balls, vacations. I was temporarily addicted to mediocrity, or as Jim Collins would put it in his book *Good to Great*, I had accepted being "good enough."

If I truly wanted to be an independent consultant, I would have to focus on the operative word *independent*, and that meant stopping what I was doing – working for someone else – and doing something new. Change. At the same time, while quitting my job with Hughes Aircraft, or Raytheon, or Enron, required ceasing the addiction of working for someone else – I would probably have to give up some of the *perceived* necessities of life while I started my own business: going out to eat, movies, paper towels, pickles, beer, cable, vacations and so on.

It wasn't until I had no choice – my job at Enron was quit for me in December 2001 – that I realized I could live without all of these things, and more, for a month, 6 months, a year…three years…while starting my own successful business. So – yes, *change* is both Impossible and Imperative. However, while this compact experience informs my perspective, this is not the core of my model. Change is all around us – in industry, government, the armed forces, and in our daily lives – at home. There's more, in the world of work:

(From *Fast Company, April 2000):* "How many of you feel uncomfortable being here? About half. Okay. Well, I hope to change that. I want all of you to be uncomfortable. Because if you're comfortable, you can't really be a revolutionary, can you?" (Ford Chairman and CEO, Bill Ford.)

(from Ward's Dealer Business, 2002): "We said in January this is a 5-year plan, and that some of the elements would take a couple of years to happen," Ford Chairman and CEO Bill Ford Jr. says during a "road show" to reassure Wall Street. "Well, of course, the world's an impatient place and everyone's saying, "Are you there yet?"

(From Ford Motor Company Press Release, Feb 2006): "Today we declare the resurgence of the Ford Motor Company. It doesn't begin today; it's already begun. But today, you'll see and hear how serious we at Ford are about winning in the 21st Century – both in North America and around the world."

Ford, like General Motors, earlier in 2006, announced the planned lay-off of 30,000 employees and the closing of three assembly plants. The first Toyotas showed up in the United States in 1957. How long does it take to *change* – in order to remain competitive on a global landscape?

But it's not just industry: Dateline WASHINGTON, Jan. 31, 2006 – President Bush said in the State of the Union Address that the United States must remain a leader on the world stage and not retreat from challenges at home and abroad, but that Americans must break a national "addiction" to oil to preserve their country's prosperity and security.

And in the Armed Forces: (From the new Chairman of the Joint Chiefs of Staff, Gen. Peter Pace, Oct 2005): "We are at war with an enemy whose publicly reiterated intent is to destroy our way of life. In response to this very real and present danger, we must execute our responsibilities with a *sustained sense of urgency.*" (my italics)

General Pace adds: "*Transformation* is a continual process, not an end state. We must transform if we are to meet future challenges. Transformation is concepts and practices, technologies and capabilities, roles and missions, organizational structures, internal processes, doctrine and education, personnel policies, and much more…

"It is as much a mindset and a culture as it is a technology or a platform and at its heart is a *willingness on the part of the individual and the organization to embrace innovation and accept analyzed risk.* We must influence both its direction and rate of change. If we do not change a single tool at our disposal, but simply change how we employ those tools, we will make significant progress in transformation." (my italics)

Change is often so difficult as to seem impossible. People talk about change incessantly…but never get around to it. It's that annual New Year's Resolution that gets recycled year after year. And so, the true core of this model is *addiction*. Each of these speakers addresses change in some form, but what each is telling us is that to *Lead* Change, to *Manage* Change, we must guide the people on our teams to cease addiction to unproductive behaviors. If it doesn't contribute to Customer Satisfaction, or to Profit, or Safety, Reliability, Durability, Quality…to Mission Accomplishment, why are we doing it?

Recipe for Success, with Seafood Buffet

Crab Legs. Shrimp. Calamari. Salmon (or Rainbow Trout). (Sea) Scallops. Plus: Tin Foil Veggies.

Ok. Take a deep breath. Focus. This is complicated. Crank up some Jimmy BUFFETT. Ice down two six-packs of a craft brew from Florida. Place 10 to 12 bamboo shish-kebab skewers in a square pan or glass baking dish. Situate another object (like a smaller baking dish) on top of the skewers before adding water (because the skewers float). Add water to the lower pan to submerge and soak the skewers for at least 20 minutes (which prevents them from turning to charcoal on the grill – later).

Ingredients

Crab and Scallops. First: This scheme requires some planning. It may also require changing the way you consider seafood on the grill (walking away from the addiction to a kitchen inside the cave). But the real lesson is in choreography. Well in advance of this weekend – seek Alaskan King Crab Legs or Snow Crab. Depending on where you live, they likely will be frozen. If you live in Goosefare Bay, Maine, or Kalifornsky, Alaska, you may have fresh crab in the local market (on the pier). The rest of us – probably – we will not. Where you will find fresh crab – you will find fresh sea scallops. If you're not getting fresh scallops at the dock, your local grocer (seafood counter) will likely have them. Two to three lbs of crab; one pound of scallops.

Shrimp: No matter where you live, drive immediately to Houma, Louisiana, and take Montegut Road (Route 55) south toward Cocodrie. You should be able to find fresh shrimp the size of your hand, from Boudreaux or Thibodeaux selling shrimp out of a 55-quart cooler alongside the highway, for exactly $4 per pound. (get two pounds – for 8 to 10 guests.) If you speak Cajun French, you might be able to haggle for a discount of 25 cents a pound.

Calamari: If you live on one of the lovely islands of Okinawa, Japan, or a nation or island bordering the Mediterranean, you may be able to find fresh squid. If you live in Chadron, Nebraska, you may need to rely on the Safeway grocery store on Morehead Street for some frozen squid. You'll need to thaw this enough to cut the (large pieces of) squid into rings. Leave the tentacle pieces uncut for the frying pan (with the calamari rings). It's easier to cut rings when the squid is almost frozen. One pound.

Salmon option: You may wish to look for wild-caught Salmon. I've had both wild-caught and farm-raised and haven't noticed a difference in taste, but the question gets down to the chemistry. Look up farm-raised versus wild-caught, and polychlorinated biphenyls (PCBs). Before I would give up farm-raised, I would look for solid empirical evidence of contamination. A good-size salmon steak filet will check in at one to two pounds.

Rainbow Trout Option: Go catch some. Four will feed a table of 8 guests (with all of this other stuff.) Scale. Clean. Remove the heads. Filet or butterfly the carcasses. Pour 2 tablespoons sesame or peanut oil in a small bowl, add two teaspoon brown sugar, one teaspoon minced fresh ginger, one teaspoon minced fresh garlic. Mix thoroughly. Brush on the trout. Set aside on a plate, covered with plastic wrap.

Directions

CRAB LEGS: You can leave these frozen until the final minutes. Rinse the crab legs for a few minutes to remove the bacteria and get rid of the crabby taste. You will, however, want to get a 2- to 3-gallon camping kettle with a medium-blue/gray enamel and those mandatory black and white (enamel) dots that don't do anything... ¾ full of water and stationed on "warm" on the outside burner of your grill if you plan to boil them. When the time comes to boil the crab legs, crank the heat up to get the water boiling. Ensure you still have ¾ of a kettle full. (If you don't have the kettle, the dots, or the external "keep your beans warm" burner on your grill...stop whining and innovate. You *can* boil crab legs inside the cave – and know that it will take a day for the aboriginal seafood odor to dissipate.) If your crab legs are red or pink, they have likely been pre-cooked and frozen by your deadly catch fishermen.

When all of your other choreography is in place, you will want to boil king crab legs 7 – 10 minutes (or... see below). smaller crab legs– 5 to 7 minutes. My recommendation is to use a tablespoon of sea salt and a tablespoon of seafood seasoning in the boil water. The alternative (changing your directions) is to soak the crab legs in sea salt and seafood seasoning – and place them on the grill (at just the right time. Roast about 15 minutes wrapped in tin foil.). Fire and maneuver. If you're cooking with charcoal (and hickory chips) this will give your crab legs a unique flavor you won't get in a restaurant!

Salmon: With the grill on medium heat, brush on teriyaki marinade or *lightly* season with your favorite season salt and coarse-ground pepper. If the skin remains – cook on the cooling rack skin side down for approximately 20-22 minutes. No need to turn. Test for done: when the meat flakes easily with a fork. (If you have skinless filets, ensure you've cleaned the grill and applied a grill-ready, high-heat non-stick spray to prevent your salmon steaks from sticking to the grill. (Or use tin foil.) Season and cook the same as above.)

Trout option: With the grill on medium heat, cook the butterflied trout on the cooling rack (top rack) for 8-10 minutes. Test for done: when the meat flakes easily with a fork.

Calamari: Depending on where you live and the support provided by your local grocer, you may find frozen squid in the frozen fish section of the meat /poultry/seafood section of your grocery store. Even if you have a local fish monger – you may find your squid frozen. If you find it fresh, locally…awesome! You still may need to cut it up into calamari size pieces. (If your local market offers prepared calamari – it's likely already cut and seasoned. Adjust accordingly.) If you're starting from scratch: easiest is to season the calamari and toss in a frying pan with olive oil. Optionally – you may wish to bread in a beer batter and deep fry:

Beer Batter: Soak the cut calamari in beer while preparing your batter. Mix one cup of flour with one to two tablespoons of Cajun seasoning: depending on the tastes of your audience. Spicy stuff.). Pour one beer into the bowl with the mixed flour and Cajun seasoning. Gently blend the flour mixture and beer into a batter, with a whisk or fork. One or two pieces of drunk calamari at a time, coat the pieces and drop into hot oil. "Done" fried calamari will have golden brown crust on the battered exterior.

Sea Scallops: These should be almost silver dollar size in diameter and ½ to ¾ inch thick (some thicker). You may either follow the above beer batter recipe, or the following shrimp routine, with butter and seasoning, teriyaki or another hypothesis.

Shrimp: Easiest – and my favorite. Two pounds of large shrimp or prawns. Peel and de-vein so your guests don't have to. If you *have* to buy your shrimp from a grocery store instead of Boudreaux' 55-quart cooler south of Houma, LA, they may or may not be peeled and de-veined. Distribute the cleaned shrimp or prawns evenly on bamboo shish-kebab skewers (previously soaked in water for 20 minutes). Brush with melted butter. Prepare to place on the grill. Three to four minutes is adequate – depending on the heat inside the closed grill. Shrimp are done when they form a "letter 'C'."

Tin Foil Veggies: Place a 2-quart mixing bowl upside down on your Norwegian pine or bamboo cutting board. Grab two sections of aluminum foil to form around the outside of the bottom of the mixing bowl – leaving 2-3 inches to spare east and west, north and south. With one section east and west; one section north and south, mold the tin foil to form to the shape of the glass bowl. Turn the entire unit over and place the aluminum foil bowl *inside* the glass mixing bowl (form the tin foil to the bowl).

Chop your favorite veggies to bite-size pieces: mushrooms, onion, zucchini, yellow squash, broccoli, pineapple, cauliflower, new (red) potatoes, carrots (carrot pieces need to be smaller as they are denser and would otherwise need to cook longer). You may also consider one inch segments of corn on the cob, eggplant or other favorite veggies. Toss veggies in a separate bowl with ½ cup of balsamic vinaigrette salad dressing (low fat – if you wish) to coat the veggies.

Dump the veggies back into the aluminum foil bowl and pull the four edges to the center. Twist to close the "bowl" and place on the grill. These will cook in about ½ hour. Leave the glass mixing bowl in the cave for someone else's adventure. If you wish to change this technique for the veggies – find a grill wok. Just remember, while you're at the wok, you're not attending to seafood. Use the wok another time.

Hypothesis

This is when you get to check the math (algebra and quantum physics) on when to start the calamari, salmon or trout, shrimp and crab legs…so that all entre options finish at precisely the same time (and the Tin Foil Veggies are done)…so that your choreography presents a Buffet Ballet.

Serve with:

Eight to twelve good friends, more amber lager, and lots more Jimmy Buffett

Simple version

Ingredients

Entre
Crab Legs
Shrimp
Calamari

Salmon (or Rainbow Trout).
(Sea) Scallops.

Directions

Crab Legs – Prepare a large enough kettle to rinse the crab legs in fresh water. Move from frozen, to rinse 2-3 times, to the grill. Roasting times will vary depending on the crab variety (size) and the actual grill temp. Try 15-20 minutes, for a recommended internal temp of 145°-150° F. To keep the moisture locked in, brush on melted butter or olive oil, sprinkle your favorite seafood seasoning, then wrap in tin foil.

Shrimp – skewer on bamboo sticks (as with shish-kebab), brush on melted butter and season lightly. Roast 3-5 minutes.

Calamari – heat olive oil, a dash of basil and a splash of chili pepper hot sauce. Fry rings and tentacles until golden brown.

Salmon or Trout – place on a sheet of tin foil. Brush on teriyaki marinade. Cook 20-22 minutes over medium heat. Fish is done when the meat flakes easily with a fork.

Recipe for Success, with Managing Change

Change leads to conflict

The easy part of this is no allegory. We already know that change causes turmoil and conflict. People don't want to change offices, learn new software, adhere to new policies. People don't want to cease addictions to unproductive work behaviors on the path to genuine 6-Sigma quality or ISO 9000 compliance. People don't want to change the way they prepare crab legs. The original 2006 essay suggests this model is about *addiction* (to unproductive or risky behaviors).

In psychotherapy terms, one model applied to the treatment of addiction – substance abuse – discusses fear: fear of the unknown, fear of not having instant gratification and the artificial stimulus supplied by alcohol, nicotine or drugs for example.

In neuro-pharmacology terms, dopamine neuro-transmitters fire to signal pleasure (the reward) – in response to sex, drugs, chocolate, finishing a marathon. Pleasure is the reward. Getting a known-quantity finished product to market is a reward. How about a *new* product?

And in behavioral psychology terms, *not* preventing unproductive work behaviors is roughly the same as rewarding productive work behaviors. Either one serves as *reinforcement*. Behaviors rewarded – reinforced – are likely to be repeated, including negative behaviors.

Now the allegory: 5th Generation Warfare. The transformation discussed in General Pace's address, in the *Change is Imperative* essay above, responds in part to what we collectively knew about where we were in the Global War on Terror in 2005. The "air-land battles" of Iraq and Afghanistan were largely over; insurgencies took hold in both.

Models of warfare evolve continuously. Debates on 4th Generation Warfare models often refer to *DIME*: Diplomacy, Intelligence, Military and Economy – in environments ranging from low- to high-intensity conflict. Fifth Generation Warfare, in contrast, approaches the integration of DIME and society. A *Fifth* Generation model takes into account cyber warfare, information operations and the non-combatant civilian populations impacted by the war, among other issues. But this is not what the battalions of current senior lieutenant colonels and colonels learned in ROTC in the late 1980s, in officer candidate school in the early 1990s. They were breast-fed on the *Leavenworth Papers* (22 of them, from 1979 through 2004), the Marine Corps' *Maneuver Warfare Handbook* (Col. Mike Wyly and William Lind, 1985) and other doctrinal and historical literature reaching back through the Cold War to the beginning of time. They learned kinetic war in a maneuver warfare generation.

Conflict leads to Change

This is where we draw lessons from the essay *and* the grill: General Pace's guidance in 2005 addressed the need for transformation in the armed forces. The conflict (war) brought on by the events of 9/11 delivered a realization, eventually, that a "fire and maneuver" strategy – alone – would not translate well to combat against terrorists and insurgents. We entered this war with a generation of professionally educated military officers who had prepared early in their careers to anticipate land-sea-air battles on the scale of World War II, with lessons from Sun Tzu, the Battle of Thermopylae, and Thucydides, and instead inherited a population-centric war with new strategies and no front lines. Fire and maneuver becomes a tactical choreography in a village or a valley instead of a strategic art covering an entire continent.

Fighting an insurgency requires an additional set of skills (with…or without the employment of tanks, artillery, air and sea power, and masses of troops): tactical, operational and strategic appreciation of the local civilian populations impacted by insurgents, such as the Taliban in Afghanistan and Pakistan who *need* the support of civil populations in order to control Afghanistan.

And now in the 21st Century, we have counter-insurgency operations ongoing in many locations around the globe. We need to understand the world – the *whole* world – like our colleagues who work in organizations like Fed-Ex, Royal Dutch Shell, Subway, Wal-Mart, the US State Department, Starbucks, or McDonalds, for example. If you want to do business in Santiago, Chile, it helps enormously to know the culture of the Santiago, Chile, business community. We need to change the way we do business.

Fire (conflict) is a catalyst for transformation – from raw seafood to grilled perfection. But crab, trout, salmon, squid and shrimp are different populations. They require different levels of heat, different seasonings, different cooking times – just as different populations in Afghanistan, or Iraq, Egypt, Somalia, Yemen… need different approaches, different choreographies.

As you train your junior leaders, remind them that the people on their teams are unique individuals, with different talents, different needs and problems, different motivations, cultures and customs. Helping your junior leaders learn to elicit from their team members the productive behaviors your organization needs to succeed (superior customer service) is an art form. If motivations are internal and incentives are external, it stands to reason that your junior leaders need to learn to read their team members in order to tailor incentives. Some people respond to cash; some to praise and recognition; and some to high-heat / high-stress jobs with significant levels of responsibility and the authority that comes with it.

Seasonings are incentives. You only need to add a little to trout or salmon to coax out the natural character, texture and flavor of the beast. Fire is the catalyst.

Change leads to conflict.

Conflict leads to change.

Marine Corps Leadership Principle

Know Yourself and Seek Self-improvement

Vol. 6 No. 6 **FOCUS** June 2010

Clowns, Jokers & Commander's Intent

Organizational buzzwords are seasonal, it seems: *transformation, innovation, diversification*. One sense of urgency replaces the next sense of urgency. Yet *QUALITY* endures, whether applied to products or services. Consciously or not, Supertramp's *The Logical Song*, on their 1979 album *Breakfast in America*, addresses the "quality" movement in American business:

> When I was young, it seemed that life was so wonderful, a miracle, oh it was beautiful, magical.
> And all the birds in the trees, well they'd be singing so happily, joyfully, playfully watching me.
> But then they send me away to teach me how to be sensible, logical, responsible, practical.
> And they showed me a world where I could be so dependable, clinical, intellectual...

Through the 1970s, we were maturing from mass production with quality measured in whole digits to programs that would eventually measure quality in parts per million...even parts per billion. Quality (and standards) "programs" (6 Sigma, ISO 9000) originally focused on quality in the private sector.

As a management consultant 8, 9, 10 years ago, I served clients on the energy, aerospace, and chemical manufacturing campuses of southeast Texas. These were – and still are – the young women and men who seek to become the Captains of Industry. And then…through the accidents of history, I was back in the Marine Corps in 2005, *back* in uniform after a 10-year hiatus.

During those 10 years in the private sector, one of the companies I observed – with those hopeful future *captains of industry* – sought to replace their middle-aged middle managers who had risen through the ranks (generally on a high school diploma) and had been promoted from within. In their place, the company planned to insert 20-somethings with MBAs. Manufactured managers with excellent business skills…but no leadership experience. Good idea or bad…how did that work out?

Some of the manufactured managers didn't do so poorly after all. Seems there are some things inherent to leadership that intuitive MBAs already know. But some failed, and they failed miserably. Why? *All* of them were stuck in the middle…with a ponderous and often invisible corporate headquarters on one side and battalions of "hourly" employees on the other. Reminds me of another '70's song:[x]

> *Well I don't know why I came here tonight,*
> *I got the feeling that something ain't right,*
> *I'm so scared in case I fall off my chair,*
> *And I'm wondering how I'll get down the stairs,*
> *Clowns to the left of me,*
> *Jokers to the right, here I am,*
> *Stuck in the middle with you.*

Captains in the Marine Corps are stuck between layers of Jokers: majors, lieutenant colonels, colonels and generals…and of course a secretary of defense, the commander in chief and ostensibly a national strategy…and the Clowns: the hordes of junior Marines who show up with little education and no experience, and who hope to work their way up from private or lieutenant to something bigger.

When you're in the parallel position in commerce – you're stuck between Jokers: directors, executive directors, vice presidents, executive vice presidents and chief executive officers with a business plan…and Clowns: the hordes who show up with little education and no experience, start at minimum wage, and focus on buying a new car and maybe a house someday…but not on your mission.

It goes like this: The Jokers read commander's intent, then give the captains a mission to execute – like "Find Osama bin Laden and defeat international terror" or "Land on Normandy Beach," or "Defeat Imperial Japan," (you're joking, right?) Or "Increase production 100%, save 50% in production costs, improve quality, and beat the next guy in customer satisfaction." (you're joking, right?)

While this is going on, the Clowns want better pay, shorter hours, longer breaks, softer beds, better food, transparent business practices, tolerance in the workplace, stock options and every parking space by the front door. "Hey! I'm a Clown! It's all about me. I have needs!"

Commander's Intent

For some, there may be an analogy in The Lord's Prayer: *Thy will be done.* Higher headquarters puts out a plan; the captains are supposed to interpret the *commander's vision for what the end result should look like, define the subordinate mission, and assign tasks and responsibilities to the Clowns.* Clowns rarely confer with Jokers. They look to their captains to explain why the company is going the direction it's going.

Commander's intent shapes the MISSION. If we don't have the mission, there's no need for the people to *execute* the mission. (If there's no market for blue widgets, no one's going to hire you to make blue widgets. If there's no need to defend our national interests overseas, there's no need for troops overseas.)

Influence

Years ago a Marine general wrote about the relationship between officers and enlisted Marines. He spoke of "father to son [or daughter] and teacher to student relationships." Now, years later – as both father and teacher, I take that lesson to my own children as well as to my junior team members. Translating Clowns for the Jokers and the Jokers for the Clowns...getting people to do things they think they don't want to do requires an advanced degree in *influence operations*. PSYOP.

How I perform as a leader shapes how my junior leaders will perform in the future. When it's my children – I tell them I'm not trying to make them *perfect children*, but better parents.

Sometimes I ask the Clowns to work harder, try again, or do something for someone else. It doesn't matter who accomplishes the mission – just that the mission is accomplished. I tell the Clowns that I will never ask them to do anything wrong, immoral, unethical or impossible. I will ask them (and show them how) to do things they've never done before. I help them find the confidence to do things they never thought they wanted to do. And for all of their hard work and sacrifices, I am obligated take their needs to the Jokers.

Recipe for Success, with Grilled Pizza Sandwich

Yes! At last! Pizza on the grill! This will take some FOCUS...

It's time for *Supertramp*...and Rafferty and Egan – *Steelers Wheel*. While you're cranking up tunes, grab a Scottish Ale. An Internet search will reveal many choices.

<u>Ingredients</u>

Pizza crust: I've used a "pancake and baking mix," general purpose flour, and ready-made frozen pizza crust. The "pancake and baking mix" seems to offer more latitude and therefore more control in contrast to the mechanically produced (and therefore mechanically predictable) frozen crust. When you make your own, you also have the option to roll and bake cheese into the edges. The cheeses *you* like. This recipe doesn't need that – as we're making a large Pizza Sandwich. Lotsa room for cheese in the middle.

4 cups pancake and baking mix, bread flour, or multi-purpose flour.

1 cup water (approx).

Toppings: Gotta know your audience.

8 ounce can tomato paste.

24 ounce jar spaghetti sauce. Lots of commercial choices, with basil, cheeses, meats, etc. Try a different hypothesis each time.

1 pound pork sausage (brown this before mounting the bottom pizza).

Pepperoni. Pre-sliced works, but you can buy a log and slice to whatever thickness you like. For one pizza, ½ pound may be enough.

Bacon. Try that "ham-like" Canadian Bacon stuff, or for grins – fry up ½ pound of thick-cut Center-Cut bacon, cut to one-inch pieces, then half-cooked and well-drained.

1 can large, pitted black olives; halved. Approx. 6 ounces dry weight.

1 onion, medium, diced or sliced. Try "sweet" onions.

1 green pepper. Washed, cleaned, sliced or diced.

1 clove elephant garlic; minced (or sliced).

½ to 1 pound fresh, whole mushrooms, sliced at home.

Seasoning – coarse-ground pepper, garlic salt…to taste.

1 cup, Mozzarella, Provolone, Parmesan and other cheeses, shredded…to taste.

Directions

Pre-heat grill to 400° F (at least 4 burners on HIGH). It is, after all, an oven…outdoors.

Two pizza crusts (do this first so the crusts can pre-bake while you're dicing and slicing): Pour the 4 cups flour in a large mixing bowl. Sprinkle one tbsp of seasoning into the flour mixture. Stir, then and add most of the water. Mix thoroughly to dough consistency. Add water as necessary to reach dough consistency. Make two loaves.

Dust flour on a large cutting board and your hands. Form one loaf into a ball, then flatten to form a crust. Flour a rolling pin and dust more flour on the dough. Roll out to form a 16-inch crust. Place this crust on a 16-inch aluminum pizza pan (the kind with a thousand little holes works great) and place on the grill with the lid closed to pre-bake for 8-10 minutes. Alternatively, find a baking stone at your local grilling store. These may be available in 12-inch or 16-inch versions. Adjust accordingly. Chop veggies while waiting, but remain focused on the timer. Return the first crust to the cave and repeat the process for the second crust.

Toppings

In a 12-inch skillet, fry the bacon pieces. Drain and reserve ¾ of the fat and place bacon on a plate with paper towel to soak up the remaining fat. Add pork sausage to residual bacon fat and brown the sausage – chopping to marble-size pieces with a spatula. Don't over-cook. Scoop out the sausage and keep the hot grease. Place bacon and sausage on a plate with a paper towel or two to *drain well.*

In the 12-inch skillet with the remaining bacon/sausage fat, add the sliced or diced onion, green pepper, garlic and mushroom (but not the black olives or pepperoni). Toss lightly on high heat for 2-3 minutes to pre-cook. Remove from heat. Collect the second crust from the grill. (Keep the grill fired up. Grab a brew and change over from *Steelers Wheel* to *Supertramp.*)

Mix the 24 ounce jar of spaghetti sauce with the 8 ounce can of tomato paste in a large bowl, then spread half of this evenly on one crust. Spread half of the shredded cheese over the sauce on one crust. Distribute toppings. If you have a request in the house for "no mushroom" or "no meat" or "no whatever," plan accordingly. Mark the edge of the crust with a knife to indicate ½ mushroom and ½ no-mushroom, for example.

After adding remaining toppings, spread remaining cheese over the toppings. Add remaining spaghetti sauce and paste over the cheese. Place the second crust on top, and place on the grill (on the pizza pan or baking stone) for an additional 12-15 minutes. (If you prefer to close the edges along the circumference, save a strip or cord of dough two fingers wide and 50.26544 inches long. Wet the edges of the crust with water (with your finger) and wrap this "cord" around the edge. Pinch to seal.) If you find 12-inch baking stones, the dough strip to seal would be 37.7 inches. (Pizza pi math)

Bake at approx 400° F. Times will vary, dependent upon the true temperature on the grill, the thickness of your pizza *sandwich,* and the desired softness or crunchiness of your crusts. Pre-baking the crusts 8-10 minutes, plus the finished pi for 12-15 minutes should do nicely. If the Ale is gettin' a wee heavy – roll over to something lighter, like a pilsner, to wash down your pizza sandwich. Slice and serve 4 to 6.

Recipe for Success, with Expeditions & Entrepreneurs

Scores of clients and students have in the past challenged me on this notion of cross-fertilizing military leadership concepts with profit-making business management theory. No overt profit motive is apparent in tactical, operational or strategic combat maneuvers; the perceived rigidity of military rank structures, and command and control seem out of place in the private sector.

Partially true on both counts. But we're still talking about organizations and the corpus of people who collectively make up and operate those organizations. And we're still talking about the role of the leaders and managers in the middle. Let's begin with the military view. In a *Small Wars Journal* article,[xi] Gomez summons Helmut von Moltke (head of the Prussian and German General Staff from 1858 to 1888):

Certainly the commander (in chief) will keep his great objective continuously in mind, undisturbed by the vicissitudes of events. But the path on which he hopes to reach it can never be firmly established in advance. Throughout the campaign he must make a series of decisions on the basis of situations that cannot be foreseen.

First off – you don't want vicissitudes anywhere near your grill, for this recipe or any other. And I don't think I've ever seen *vicissitudes* in any recipe book. But stuff happens. Stuff happens in the private sector and stuff happens in combat. As Gomez points out: "The plan changes but the [overall] objectives do not unless the mission changes."…and further: "Every commander and every staff must be prepared to use diligence in dealing with temporary setbacks and unanticipated obstacles…they must remain rigidly focused on the end-state, but creatively flexible in how the…end-state is reached." Von Moltke concludes:

The successive acts of war are thus not premeditated designs, but on the contrary are spontaneous acts guided by military measures. Everything depends on penetrating the uncertainty of veiled situations to evaluate the facts, to clarify the unknown, to make decisions rapidly, and then to carry them out with strength and constancy. (von Moltke, 1871)

So. If strategic leaders at corporate headquarters for Boeing, JC Penney, Wal Mart, Starbucks, Southwest Airlines, Johnson and Johnson, General Motors and so on, and so on – are trying to control tactical operations, they're not doing their job. But if they are not aware of *vicissitudes* at the tactical level, the captains…the leaders and managers in the middle…aren't doing *their* job. Gomez writes on the art of Assessment. It is the front-line manager or tactical commander who must learn to evaluate pop-up situations and respond rapidly and confidently, guided by the operating culture of the organization and with an eye on the end-state or strategic objective. (They have to be given the authority to do so and they should be keeping their seniors informed.)

This is the expeditionary nature of Marines: Receive a mission and commander's intent; plan; execute; and prepare to change plans based on the operational realities on the ground. Revolutions in technology in our own generation not only support this in both the private sector and in combat, these revolutions in the speed and volume of information needed to support instant decision-making at the point of impact make centralized command and decentralized control a *necessity*. And – the front-line leader needs to keep strategic leaders <u>and</u> the troops informed.

On the business end, Peter Drucker has much to say:

The manager is a servant. His or her master is the institution being managed and the first responsibility must therefore be to it. The manager's first task is to make the institution, whether business, hospital, school or university, perform the function and make the contribution for the sake of which it exists…The manager who uses a position at the head of a major institution to become a public figure…while the company or university erodes through neglect, is not a statesman, but is irresponsible and false to his trust.[xii]

See Jim Collins' discussion on Lee Iacocca, in *Good to Great,* page 29. Collins writes on developing a culture of leadership. Iacocca turned Chrysler around, but didn't leave a stable of "next leaders" in his wake. When Iacocca left, Chrysler again foundered.[xiii] Drucker's view is that the manager's first duty is to the organization – and by extension, to the organization's mission.

Who then is responsible for the troops? Who keeps the troops informed about tactical operations?

Marines (and soldiers, sailors and airmen) have something genuinely impossible to find in the private sector: non-commissioned officers – NCOs. The senior enlisted member of a military organization (a first sergeant, sergeant major, etc.) serves as the advisor to a commander on all issues related to enlisted Marines. As most of the heavy lifting in combat is accomplished by enlisted Marines (roughly 91 percent of the Marine Corps), this is no small task. The working relationship between the company commander (front-line manager) and his or her senior enlisted Marines (Staff NCOs) must be a relationship based on a significant level of trust.

But if there are no NCOs in the private sector, how will they ever succeed?

Southwest Airlines offers a model worthy of emulation in the private sector. In *Southwest Airlines from an organizational perspective,* analyst Jurjan Knol observes:

So what exactly is the secret behind the success of Southwest Airlines?...The real magical trick seems to be the way SWA is able to motivate its employees, so they in turn are able to give the customers a better product. Three important factors can be identified how SWA manages to keep the spirit high. First, the relationship between management and workforce. There is a real family relationship amongst the entire workforce, so everybody feels very much involved and responsible. Second, training at the "University for People" decreases hierarchical thinking because everybody gets the same basic training and everybody learns the culture and values of Southwest Airlines....Third, Herb Kelleher, one of the founders and now chairman of the Board, is an important leader for the company. His vision, humor and hands-on mentality are very inspiring for all employees at Southwest Airlines.[xiv]

How is Southwest perpetually successful? Their publicly stated priorities are: Employees come first, Customers second, and Stockholders third. The end result is that employees who are treated special treat their customers as special. This perspective describes the Marine Corps in so many ways. There may not be "non-commissioned officers" in the private sector, but organizations that invest heavily in developing, jealously maintaining, and teaching their organizational culture are chronically more successful than those that do not. Delegating decision-making authority to the lowest possible levels contributes to Marines accomplishing a variety of missions. The Corps' history is fat with charismatic leaders – but leaders, as servants, devoted to the organization and its missions.

In the end – that expeditionary mindset in Marines translates easily into Drucker's passion for entrepreneurship: innovation and marketing. Invent and sell. Few organizations on the planet do a better job of selling their organization than the Marine Corps (thanks both to Marine Corps successes in combat and to the commercial producers of Marine Corps advertising – J. Walter Thompson (JWT). JWT is another story, but the entrepreneurial spirit in the Corps (a non-profit organization) is likewise as worthy of emulation as Southwest Airlines.

What's the point? Profit motive is not the first focus. Southwest Airlines knows that when they select and train the best people in their industry – profit will be an end result. Convert "profit" to *mission accomplished* and the same concept holds true in the Corps. (Drucker was philosophically aligned with this mindset, and I agree. Profit is a derivative of superior products and customer service; both are derivatives of superior people.) Yes – "the mission comes before the man" in the Marine Corps, but the Corps trains Marines in teamwork so well, that the mission becomes an inevitable result of well-trained teams, of people who believe in the mission.

Knol's brief article on SWA addresses the final characteristic in common with the Marine Corps: "…There is a real family relationship amongst the entire workforce, so everybody feels very much involved and responsible." In the

Corps – this is expressed in the bumper sticker moniker: *We Few, We Proud, We Band of Brothers.*

Captains are no longer stuck in the middle but are the middle brothers and sisters – the negotiators and diplomats, and the Clowns and Jokers are bound by a common goal.

Marine Corps Leadership Trait: **Unselfishness**
Marine Corps Leadership Principle:
Develop a sense of responsibility among your subordinates

(If this chapter in particular causes the reader to stand up in the aisle of a Southwest Airlines flight from Washington, DC, to Tampa, FL, while the seatbelt light is on and scream, "THIS is ALL THEORY!!! There IS NO FAMILY ATMOSPHERE in AMERICAN organizations!!! ...the writer reminds the reader that the Grilling Studio stuck-in-the-middle-with-you portion of each chapter is specifically focused on trial and error, new hypotheses, experimentation. The reader's response is probably a reaction to a current reality. That's understandable. Just lay down on the couch and tell me: How does this make you feel?)

Building a "family atmosphere" takes years. Hard work. Patience. Giving. Planning. Sacrifice...like marriage.

Vol. 2 No. 7 **FOCUS** July 2006

July 4th & the 2nd Law of Thermodynamics

Independence Day is Freedom Day.

Think in terms of your job. If you have a job, you're fortunate. If you don't *need* to work, you may or may not be even more fortunate. If you're self-employed – Independent – you likely have to bust your 6 to run your own business, but the *Independence* is rewarding. Either way, you're Free to work. Every once in a while I run into someone who thinks the latter means "free to come and go...but not get much work done." The *quality* we experience in Freedom or Independence comes at a cost.

Robert Pirsig reveals his epiphany in *Zen and the Art of Motorcycle Maintenance,* that *freedom* is a precursor to *quality.* Continuously improved quality derives from innovation, creativity, and flexibility. Individually, and as organizations, we must have *freedom* to create quality, in missions accomplished, or products and services. Fewer laws and regulations lead to more innovation; greater opportunity for the entrepreneur. What if we could export the concept of *freedom* as *quality* to every member of our teams? Would they line up to buy in...perhaps through payroll deduction? What if *ideas* could become more evenly distributed?

One of my favorite places to browse on the Internet has been the Principia Cybernetica Web Project (PCP). Enter the

2nd Law of Thermodynamics. (*Real* engineers bristle at the application of the canonical laws of physics to human dynamics. I ain't skeered.) Paraphrased from Wikipedia, the 2nd Law of Thermodynamics tells us that "in a system made up of quantities of matter, its pressure, density and temperature differences all tend to equalize over time. The system's *entropy*, which increases with this process, is a measure of how far the equalization has progressed. For example, take a *system* consisting of a cup of hot water in a cool room. Over time the water will tend to cool and evaporate, and the room will warm up slightly. The system's heat has become more evenly distributed, and thus the entropy of the cup of water and the room (as a system) has increased."

Not surprisingly, there is a parallel concept called *Social Entropy*. From the PCP web project at http://pespmc1. vub.ac.be/ASC/SOCIAL_ENTRO.html: "...a measure of the natural decay of the structure, or of the disappearance of distinctions within a social system. Much of the energy consumed by a social organization is spent to maintain its structure, counteracting social entropy." To avoid having your system diluted by contrary values, <u>demonstrate and export better quality values</u>. Entropy is *disorder and conflict*.

One employee's expression of the freedom to do, say or wear anything he or she *wants* – or show up for work anytime he or she wants – is a cup of cold water splashed into the relatively warmer room of a corporate whole. Organizations expend enormous energy (capital) to prevent decay and devolution...to keep the heat on. Our Founding Fathers started a really good deal, leaving behind the concept that "We hold these truths to be self-evident, that all men are created equal, that they are endowed by their Creator with certain unalienable Rights, that among these are Life, Liberty and the pursuit of Happiness…" and a Bill of Rights. What they didn't leave us is a Bill of Responsibilities.

On the scale of a *holy grail*, one of the transcendent goals of leadership is to develop team members who can operate autonomously…independently. But this requires teaching the difference between inalienable *rights* and earned *privileges*. This requires teaching that Independence – our Liberty and Freedoms – come with some responsibilities. Parents seek to provide their children with enough guidance in both rules *and* values so that their children can operate on autopilot when they reach maturity.

Corporate leaders seek to impose order through written ISO 9000 processes or Six Sigma-like *Quality* programs, while demonstrating corporate values such as *customer focus* and *treating all employees with dignity, courtesy and respect* as guides to human performance and the enlightened paths to profitability.

Nations and even nation-less entities with the economic and military might to operate as global or regional leaders seek to influence other nations through the export of political, ideological or economic systems, like *democracy, socialism, terrorism* or *capitalism,* which are all encumbered with laws as well as values.

The unwritten expectation in each of these cases is that subordinates will do what you want them to do – and ultimately return some social or economic benefit. The truth is, everyone seeks to arrange and rearrange the world around them to suit their needs. We do it with our mates, our cars, clothing and homes. We do it at a community level and we do it at the state and national levels. People like *freedom,* but rebel against the laws and policies. My Pursuit of Happiness may clash with yours. Howard Stern loves his 1st Amendments Rights. I love Howard Stern's 1st Amendment Rights too – because they're the same as mine. It all boils down to the quest for *freedom*. No one likes to be restrained, held against their will. But Rights come with Responsibilities.

In quest of the deeper meaning of *responsibility*, I searched Wikipedia for the term *stewardship* and found this general comment (meaning there are no articles specifically focused on the metaphysical "stewardship."): "In general **stewardship** is responsibility for taking good care of resources entrusted to one."

We make much of the concept of taking care of resources in the United States (and I'm feeling a little bit Andy Rooneyish here...) – but folks do talk about this stuff. We have natural resources, like water, oil and coal, minerals such as gold, silver and bauxite, land (which the U.S. has much of), forests and so on. And – in every organization this book reaches – there is likely a department or division called "Human Resources" or some logical equivalent. People *are* our greatest tangible resource, and collectively we own *Freedom* as our greatest intangible. It's been entrusted to us. If we want to continue to own it, we've got to take good care of it.

Recipe for Success, with Stuffed Peppers

Sure – you could use an oven, but *sensitive dependence on initial conditions* suggests that if you cook your stuffed peppers on the GRILL, if your stuffed peppers are *tested by fire,* you'll get a better product. Flexibility means you can start with green bell peppers, or the sweeter red, yellow or orange variety (sweeter than the green because they're left on the plant longer to sun-ripen). Bell peppers are cousins to the "hot" tasting chili pepper; they just lack the chemical that causes the hot taste. On successive outings, test a range of ingredients (hypotheses) – like ground beef, pork sausage, or perhaps chopped shrimp – in a base of white, brown or wild rice. This hypothesis starts with the basics:

Servings: 5

Prep Time: 30 Minutes

Cooking Time: 30 minutes

<u>Ingredients</u>

1 cup white rice

5 bell peppers. Select large, fairly symmetrical fruits that can hold plenty of stuffing and stand on their own on the grill.

½ onion, diced

1 lb ground beef – 80%, or 85%, or 93% or 97% lean: to taste

1 tbsp minced garlic (2-3 cloves)

1cup diced mushroom

3 tbsp olive oil

3 tbsp soy sauce

Directions

Turn on some sports, or find some classical music – like Def Leppard, Steve Miller Band, Jethro Tull, Aerosmith, Dire Straits. Find a cold German beer.

White Rice: You should be able to prep all of the other ingredients while the rice is cooking. In a 2-quart sauce pan (with a lid), bring 2 cups of water to boiling, then add the 1 cup of rice. Turn the heat to the lowest setting; put the lid on the pan; set a timer for 22 minutes. (When the timer goes off… take the rice off the heat and set aside with the lid on.)

Peppers: Wash the bell peppers before chopping / dicing. Cut the tops off of the peppers – enough to form a bowl for the stuffing. Cut the remaining fruit from around the stem and add this to the onion, garlic and mushroom, below.

Ground beef: While the rice is cooking, heat the olive oil and soy sauce in a 10-inch skillet over medium heat. When the soy sauce starts to sputter in the olive oil – it's hot. Add the ground beef in order to brown it, but don't over-cook.

Stuffing: While the rice is cooking and the ground beef is browning, if it's after 5, grab another beer, a cutting board, a chef's knife and the onion, garlic, mushroom and the bell pepper from the tops. Check on the ground beef. Dice the onion, garlic, mushroom and bell peppers from the tops. Check on the ground beef. Chop and mix all of the onion, garlic, mushroom and bell pepper together (from the tops). Set aside in a bowl.

Prep: Drain the juice from the ground beef into a bowl. (You'll need this juice in a moment.) Add the recently chopped and blended onion, garlic, mushroom and bell pepper – and integrate with the ground beef using a spatula.

Ding! The rice is done. Turn off the rice, run out back and fire up your grill. If you're using charcoal, wood or pellets - all better than gas, but gas gets the job done just fine - you should have run out back to fire up (pre-heat) your grill ten minutes ago, when you got that beer. We'll cook the peppers with indirect heat (around 250° F).

Back to Prep: Back in the cave, add the rice to the browned ground beef and chopped vegetables; blending with the spatula. Thoroughly mixed, spoon into the waiting bell peppers. Press the mixture firmly to fill all those voids in the pepper. Spoon the drippings/juice from the ground beef/soy sauce/olive oil into the stuffed peppers. This helps the stuffing remain moist on the grill.

On the Grill

If, for example, you have a four-burner grill: turn off two burners and set the other two on lowest setting. Arrange the stuffed peppers on the side without direct heat. All grills are different – testing various hypotheses, you may find it necessary to place a tin foil shield between the peppers and the heated side of the grill. If grilling with charcoal push your coals to one side of the grill base, replace the grill and cook the stuffed peppers on the other side.

Cook for 30 minutes. Cook 20 minutes for a firmer bell pepper shell.

<u>Serve with:</u>

Four other people. It's a complete meal in itself, but you may wish to add a dash of Worcestershire Sauce, steak sauce, BBQ sauce or soy sauce. It's a light meal, so add a lager beer, or a cabernet or merlot. If it's just you and the missus – play Barry White. You may think it sucks – but she loves it.

Simple version

Prepare scratch rice – boil 2 cups water. When water reaches a rolling boil, add rice and set stove to lowest setting. Set timer to 22 minutes.

Brown the ground beef, with soy sauce and olive oil. Reserve juices.

Chop the veggies. Add the veggies to the browned meat. Add the rice and blend completely on low heat. Avoid over-cooking (it's all going to the grill). Stuff the peppers.

Place a sheet of tin foil on one side of the top rack of the grill. Place all stuffed peppers on the tin foil. Add the reserved juices to moisten the filling. Light the opposite side of the grill and roast for 20-30 minutes.

Recipe for Success, with Junior Leaders

If this recipe were an ancient Aztec allegory (*capsicum annuum* are native to Mexico, Central and South America), it should be no stretch to see the pepper as your protégé – the junior leaders you train. Someone's got to hold it all together.

Sensitive dependence on initial conditions goes all the way back to where, when and how your leaders were socialized. Not only do we get the diversity of different colors and varied tastes, some junior leaders have already been tested by fire – growing up in inner cities, serving in combat in Iraq or Afghanistan, or growing up in challenging, dysfunctional families.

Unless you plant your own garden, you likely browse what the grocer offers. You get the end – or interim – result of someone else's nurturing. Likewise, whether you're molding leaders for the private sector, the armed forces, a government position or academia...someone else delivered Junior Leader to your doorstep partially trained. Already partly screwed up.

Sensitive dependence on initial conditions? You have a diverse array of incoming freshmen to turn into leaders. It doesn't really matter if they're green...or red, yellow or orange. The underlying principles of leadership will unite them and serve them well in each unique assignment. Despite their diversity – they will each respond to trials by fire.

That diverse array of raw material also means they are all different, and – if all different, there is no such thing as *perfect*. (Perfect only happens once.) There *can* be a best in class, class after class, whether second lieutenant, new MBA, four-star general, dean, deacon or CEO. The constants of Leadership have never said: "Apply only to green leaders. Or only yellow, or orange or red."

As for that stuffing in your bell peppers...you may have by now considered that to be what we stuff their intellect with. OK. But the stuffing is protected by the bell pepper shell. That stuffing might also be their team members – encircled and wrapped up in the protection of the team leader. Who's going to take the heat when the stuff hits the fan?

Vol. 8 No. 1 **FOCUS** January 2012

Knock three times...

Every once in a while, the *Oldies* radio station plays that 1970 bubblegum rock tune *Knock Three Times* (on the ceiling if you want me). Written by Irwin Levine and L. Russell Brown and recorded by Tony Orlando and Dawn, the song offered an innocent plea, in a time of bell-bottoms, big hair and war protests songs. As an *Oldie* it serves as a metaphor for both the differences and the similarities between the world of civilians and the smaller world of the uniformed military.

In a different, more contemporary radio world: If we are to believe the self-appointed radio mouthpieces for the conservative half of the nation, our nation is beset with an entitlement mentality. Clearly articulated by these radio talk show hosts is the notion that those who feel *entitled* are that portion of the population who pay little or no income tax, or who collectively are represented by the likes of *Occupy Wall Street*-ers, or are embodied in the rioting Greeks (and other Europeans) who demand higher pay, government subsidies, free medical care and retirement at the age of 55.

This entitlement generation is certainly real (and the radio mouthpieces are correct), and it's been building for more than a generation, but this is not the target population for this essay. There is another, insidious, kind of entitlement and it's a badge worn by some percentage of people in leadership positions.

Imagine the following notice, posted at eye-level, by the doors of each manager, director or vice president in corporate America:

PROCEDURE FOR ENTERING OFFICE:

1. Knock (3 times, using palm of hand).

2. Wait for permission to enter.

3. Enter. Stand at attention facing forward.

4. Sound off, last name, rank, unit: "Reporting as ordered, Sir."

5. When acknowledged, state your business.

6. When finished, state: "Request permission to carry on, Sir."

7. Granted permission, about face, depart and state: "Aye-Aye, Sir."

In an almost quaint way, this harkens back to an earlier, slightly more regimented era in America's armed forces. This ritual is generally out-dated in the armed forces of the 21st century, except perhaps in basic training ("boot camp") or select schools like the Navy's BUDS (basic underwater demolition school – the door to SEAL training) or the Army's Ranger School. Students at the school I served, in uniform, in 2005-'08 merely knock once or twice *as* they open the door to an instructors' bullpen (without waiting for permission) and announce, "Student on deck." Either way, still an alien concept in our federal, state or local governments; non-profits; or civilian universities.

And of course, we likely wouldn't find this "knock three times" notice at the door of any manager, director or vice president in America's private sector. But what *do* we find?

In both cases – knocking on the ceiling, or three times at the leader's door – the issues are communication and accessibility. Relegating the communication between boyfriend and girlfriend to the oldies radio station, our focus is on organizational communication and instilling a particular attitude in junior leaders. In the Marine Corps, when a corporal is selected for promotion to sergeant, it's not a reward for having been a superior corporal – it's a selection based on the corporal's apparent aptitude to perform at the next senior level of responsibility. There's a huge difference. The corporal who feels he or she is *entitled* to a promotion would be mistaken. From the moment the corporal pinned on his corporal rank insignia, he was training to become a sergeant. Likewise, the former governor, senator, congressman or businessman or woman who feels he or she is entitled to become President of the United States is also mistaken.

And so, what of leaders in the private sector? Let the debate begin: Managers manage production, processes and costs. Managers organize and plan, direct and control resources. Leaders lead people. Managers may lead, and leaders may manage, but *leadership* exclusively addresses relationships between people. Leaders take us into uncharted territory. Management is an occupation. Leadership is a privilege.

In addition to Tony Orlando, bell bottoms and big hair, another phenomenon from the 1970s was the philosophy of *Management by Wandering Around* (or *Walking Around*). A leader who feels entitled to his position may also feel that all of those people on his team work for him. A leader with that kind of entitlement attitude may feel that the people on his team need to come to him, ask permission to speak (equivalent to "getting on the calendar"). He would be mistaken. A little humility goes a long way.

My junior leaders need to be 4X4 leaders – 4-wheel drive leaders – who can get around obstacles. My junior leaders need to serve their teams, kick down doors for their teams and ensure they have the tools and resources they need to accomplish their missions. My junior leaders need to be thankful for the opportunity to demonstrate an aptitude for greater responsibility. And my junior leaders need to learn how to hire experts, cut 'em loose and avoid micromanaging.

What these junior leaders are *entitled to* are pay and benefits (work is a transaction), and senior leaders who serve them with the same humility.

Recipe for success, with Up-Armored Brown Sugar Meat Loaf

Prep time: 20 minutes

Cooking time: 1 hour

Ready in: 1 hour 30 minutes

<u>Ingredients</u>

½ cup packed brown sugar

½ cup ketchup

1 ½ lbs lean ground beef

¾ cup milk

2 eggs

1 ½ tsp salt

¼ tsp ground black pepper

1 small onion, chopped

¼ tsp ground ginger

¾ cup finely crushed saltine cracker crumbs

<u>Prep</u>

West Pointers preheat oven to 350° F (175° C for Air Force Academy Grads. For Naval Academy grads – it's 450° Kelvin. For Texas A&M graduates…it's really, really hot.)

Lightly grease a 5X9 inch loaf pan. (Marines are authorized to use a pan, loaf, 9X5 inch – if a 5X9 is not available.)

Directions

Press the brown sugar in the bottom of the prepared loaf pan and spread the ketchup over the sugar.

In a mixing bowl, mix thoroughly all remaining ingredients and shape into a loaf. Place on top of the ketchup.

Bake in pre-heated oven for 1 hour or until juices are clear.

Serve hot.

Serves eight

Recipe for Success, with Metaphors & Allegories

Some readers might take Jack Nicholson as the image of a Marine colonel, through his chilling portrayal of Colonel Jessup in the film *A Few Good Men*: ("You can't handle the truth…"). I've worked with a few hundred colonels in the past 40 years and have only met one "Colonel Jessup-like" character on active duty. Nicholson actually pulled off a fairly convincing colonel, but understanding why Nicholson's character is a caricature requires an internalized understanding of the broader culture of the Marine Corps. The challenge with these things – allegories – of course, is that not all readers can relate to the antecedents in a bucket of metaphors and allegories. For an audience with a significant majority with no experience or interest in things military, explaining the military in a page or two is likely pointless.

Suggesting that the senior welders or shop supervisors are akin to the "NCOs" of a commercial metal fabrication plant requires an explanation of the duties, culture, training and experience of military non-commissioned officers. That too is impossible or pointless – in two pages. But perhaps it's not necessary. According to a 2011 Pew Research poll, no more than .5 percent of the US population has been in the armed forces at any given time since 2001. In contrast, close to 10 percent of the US population served on active duty during most of World War II. In real numbers, that's about 1.5 million of 300 million in 2010, and about 12 million of 135 million during WW II. The point is – I acknowledge the military references may not apply to every understanding.[xv]

And so – we move through this kind of exercise with a measure of caution and apprehension, and understand that some messages will fail to resonate with some readers. A parallel responsibility guides the professor in a classroom (teaching one concept to 20 graduate students with 20 different reference points – using a single metaphor. It doesn't often work; the professor may need to explain a complex concept in several different ways.)

Likewise the private sector leader seeking to develop leadership skills in that new crop of junior leaders may discover that someone in your company's offsite team building exercise, in a leased hotel conference room, will not actually care who moved his cheese. It may be even more likely, as the years tick by, that up-and-coming leaders may have missed *The Wizard of Oz;* Dorothy's experiences in *The OZ Principle* won't resonate. These and other models are still good models, but it's essential to know your audience.

The core of developing leadership skills is education and training. Our junior leaders may be *junior* but they are still adults. The godfather of adult education theory in the US through the past half century was Malcom Knowles. Chief among his contributions was *The modern practice of adult education: From pedagogy to andragogy.*[xvi] Among the principles manifest in Knowles' adult learning theory are the assumptions that adults:

1   need to know why they need to learn something
2   need to learn experientially
3   approach learning as problem-solving
4   learn best when the topic is of immediate value

With regard to the second of these assumptions, *experience* – including mistakes – provides the basis for learning activities. Fundamentally, experience also serves as the grounding for metaphors and allegories, similes and analogies. Explaining that negotiating Philadelphia's city traffic is analogous to driving in downtown Boston…to an audience of 10-year-olds is pointless. Yet it may also be pointless for adults who have never driven in Boston or…who are not planning to drive in Philadelphia. It may be a fact, based on experience, but what's the point?

In contrast to *pedagogy*, in which teachers deliver "content," instruction for adult learners – including instruction in leadership – should focus more on the process of learning than on a volume of facts. Adults learn better with metaphors than do children specifically because they have a broader base of experiences. With this knowledge, seniors in an organization take on the role of facilitator rather than judge or lecturer, and succeeding trips to the grill serve as case studies and simulations. You want your junior leaders to be able to operate as leaders – without a cookbook. In other words, you can memorize leadership traits and principles – but that rote memory doesn't make you a leader. The models and metaphors in this book are designed to illustrate situations in which those traits and principles have meaning.

Innovation

= Season to taste. No matter how much instruction senior leaders provide to emerging leaders, some people will change the recipe – either to suit their own tastes (and experiences) or to respond to new circumstances. Leadership development is about principles, with very few facts or laws.

When it comes to brown sugar and meatloaf, I wouldn't try this chapter's recipe on anyone. Someone sent me the recipe; I thanked him and went on about my business. Meatloaf is a metaphor for steak. Our leaders – raw meat – come with a wide range of knowledge and skills. Some are steaks; some are ground beef – already run through a grinder. And grilling is a metaphor for leadership.

I have my own recipe for meatloaf. It's called Porterhouse. Sear the top and bottom on high heat (about a minute each side), then move off the direct fire for 3-5 minutes per side (depending on the thickness of your steak) – for hot rare to medium rare beef.

Marine Corps Leadership Principle:
Employ your people and your team in accordance with their capabilities
Marine Corps Leadership Trait
Knowledge

Vol. 2 No. 3 # FOCUS March 2006

Nobody is important

Recalled to active duty in 2005…checking back into a uniformed world (and blending as silently as possible through the membrane), it was nearly impossible to determine which was the Land of Oz – that commercial, civilian world I had temporarily put on the shelf or the camouflaged reality I had returned to.

It helps to have an avatar.

My guide came in the form of a girl, perhaps 10 to 12 years old, staying with her parents at the Guest Quarters on the Navy base where I was working. Headed to the elevator in desert camouflage, my work uniform, I was intercepted by this young lady. Her father was probably a Navy officer because my uniform was apparently unfamiliar to her.

She caught up to me at the elevator, ahead of her parents, and asked, "What are you?"

"I'm a Marine Captain," I replied, "And what are you?"

"I'm a nobody," she replied. (Cute – and perhaps predictable from a 'tweener, who's no longer a small child dreaming of becoming an astronaut, a babysitter, a vet and a movie star all at the same time, and not yet a late teenager with eyes on college, the stock market, the State Department or the bar exam.)

"Excuse me, Young Lady," I said. "Are you an American?"

"Yes sir! Of course!"

"And do you love the United States of America?"

"Of course!"

"Then you're not a *nobody*…you are a Patriot."

She smiled, broadly, and skipped back down the hall to announce to her parents that she was a Patriot – as if she had just been knighted. I never saw the young lady again, or her family, but this girl had planted a marker. Improved my focus.

The week I left Houston, headed for a Marine Corps base, I heard on the radio about one of our local businessmen who, with his wife, had supplied a furnished home for a year for the family that had just been blessed with identical quadruplets. Despite his wealth, "Mattress Mac" is humble, gives much to his community, and sees his community and his country as something bigger than himself. He too is a Patriot. Another marker.

You don't have to wear the uniform – or *ever* have worn the uniform – to be a patriot.

Our challenge, as leaders in the middle and even in the leading roles in our organizations, is to help our junior team members internalize and integrate the understanding of their own worth with that concept of being part of *something bigger than themselves.*

The target, of course, is patriotism. Organizational Patriotism. Coke and Pepsi have made something of a commercial comedy about this, with the Coke delivery guy getting caught drinking Pepsi (or was it the Pepsi guy drinking a Coke?)

National patriotism is fairly easy to understand. Regional pride, ethnic pride, pride in a college or local football team or baseball team...all of these are understandable too. People display their state flag, college teams and national colors on their cars, on ball caps and T-shirts and just about anything that will carry a logo.

But Organizational Patriotism? Do your team members wear the company logo during their off hours? Can you imagine one of your junior team members getting into a protracted debate with a competitor over whose company is best? Over whose company sells the best quality product? Provides the best customer service? Treats its employees best? Has the best benefits? Best working environment? Best leaders? Best internal communication? Best HR department? Really think about this. If not – *why* not?

(So... where do I start?) In simple terms, organizational pride – patriotism – is a *meaning* or set of beliefs that derive from your culture. It's an identity. Pride is manifest in behavior and language. If you have a morale challenge in your organization, behavior and language are likely devoid of organizational pride and patriotism.

Culture may be thought of as the sum of *symbols, rituals* and *myths*. Your organization's symbols should be everywhere...on hats, lunch boxes, bumper stickers, key chains, coffee cups – the kinds of things you can find in any logo-happy sports store trying to get you to spend $85 for a football jersey with number 35 on it. Pass around your logo *freely*. There is psychology to this. People justify, mentally, but perhaps subconsciously, *why* they are wearing your company's logo shirt to the mall on a Saturday afternoon – instead of a football jersey with #35 on it.

Myths are the stories of your company's successes. The crucible of your organization's successes includes the veterans – the retired employees who overcame adversity. Bring them in to tell their stories. Often. They are wisdom embodied. Rituals also carry meaning. These are team rally events to celebrate the delivery of a major project. Raising and lowering the company flag each day is a ritual. Retirements and promotions are rituals, as are celebrations of new customers. Write a company anthem.

Then…celebrate Nobody. Let Nobody carry the company flag. Instill pride in Nobody. Guide Nobody to organizational patriotism.

Recipe for Success, with Hamburgers & World-Famous Potato Salad

This is, obviously, all about loyalty. Patriotism invokes Independence Day and all things Americana – like football, hamburgers and apple pie.

Select an all-American beer to go with all-American tunes: ice down a case of brewed-in-Texas beer. There are several.

If Bock – dial up some Kansas, or more Willie Nelson. If Blonde – spin the Beach Boys.

Fire up the grill. It needs to be *hot*.

Start the water a-boilin' for hard-boiled eggs and the potatoes. If you submerge the eggs after the water reaches a rolling boil, 12 minutes will do. Move to iced water as soon as they're done; they'll be easier to peel. Potatoes diced to "dice" size will cook to 'firm and done" in about 5-7 minutes. (It generally helps to boil each separately (the eggs and the potatoes, not each diced potato). Someone from Texas A&M will call me on this.

Ingredients

Burgers

1 lb. ground beef (or turkey) per 3 hamburgers

1 onion, diced or sliced. (finely diced folded into the ground beef, OR sliced – on top after grilling). If diced – fold half into the ground beef; save the other half for the potato salad.

1 tbsp steak sauce, Worcestershire sauce or fav BBQ sauce per pound

Sliced cheese – American, Provolone or Mozzarella work nicely

Buns: Fresh sourdough buns from the bakery

Condiments: sliced onion, tomato, lettuce, pickles, ketchup, hot sauce, avocado, mushrooms, sweet, hot or yellow mustard, mayonnaise – to taste

Potato Salad

Potatoes: This is a matter of taste, too. I use 5 lbs. of white baking potatoes, push them through a manual "French Fries" slicer, then dice to a bit smaller than Las Vegas dice. You may like new (red) 'taters or some other version. The basic idea is to take the extra step and dice the potatoes to genuinely bite-sized pieces. (Have you ever gone to someone else's family reunion and discovered potato salad with golf ball-size pieces of potato.) The flavor comes from the "dressing," and smaller pieces provide more surface area for the seasoned mayonnaise.

Onion: The other half of that – diced.

8 eggs, hard-boiled; each egg cut to 8 pieces.

6 to 10 kosher dill pickles, cut to bite-size pieces

Mayonnaise – about 4 to 6 heaping tablespoons, with your eyes closed. My Grill Friend recommends low-fat mayo. Sometimes I just divide the ingredients and make a regular batch and a low-fat batch. Mayonnaise with olive oil has 4 grams of fat per serving compared to 10 or 11g per serving from real mayonnaise.

Add a bit of milk to the mayonnaise. Use a whisk with the milk to cut the mayo and reduce the consistency so it coats the potatoes, hard-boiled eggs, onion and pickles. The goal is a consistency akin to thick, rich "Ranch Dressing" you'd pour out of a bottle.

Seasons: To taste. My home blend is a mix of salts and peppers, various blends of season salts and coarse ground pepper – therefore: S'neason Salt. Add seasoning to the mayo while blending.

Directions

World Famous Potato Salad

Boil the potatoes. Boil the eggs. (When cooled, and peeled, cut the eggs to bite-size pieces – like 8 pieces per egg. That's ½, three times.) Dice the pickles and onion.

Mix the mayo and milk, then add S'neason Salt and mix thoroughly with a whisk. Fold in boiled potatoes, hard-boiled eggs and onion in the mayo mix. Sometimes, we add a single tablespoon of yellow mustard to the mayo mix.

To cool – place the World Famous Potato Salad in the fridge in the garage, in a large mixing bowl, covered perhaps with tin foil or a plastic wrap cover to keep the oxygen out of the salad and the amazing smells out of the beer in the fridge in the garage.

Burgers

Add a tablespoon of steak sauce or Worcestershire sauce and 1-2 tbsp of diced onion (per pound) to ground beef.

You know the drill…You can find ground beef from 75% lean to 93% or 94% lean. You know the taste and the consequences.

For 1 pound, form 6 equal-size (small) patties. Place one slice of cheese on a patty, then another patty on top of the cheese. Pinch the edges around the perimeter and reform the patty. Repeat as necessary for 1/3 lb. burgers. If you have a no-cheese request, just delete the cheese, please. (One pound – 16 ounces – divided by 6 = "small patties" of 2.66 ounces. Once you place a slice (or two) of American cheese and add another 2.66-ounce hamburger patty – you get a rather large "hamburger.")

Super Supper Time

If, for example, you desire a medium rare burger with melted cheese in the middle, grill the burgers on the top rack (over high heat) approximately 5 minutes on the first side and approximately 3 to 3 ½ minutes on the opposite. Internal temperature recommendation for ground beef is 140° F.

Place (hamburger) buns, insides facing the heat, on the top rack when you flip the burgers. Keep an eye on those buns. Three minutes may be more than enough. Try 2-3 minutes on the first hypothesis.

Top with lettuce, avocado, tomato, onion, condiments

Serve with:

A Texas beer, Word Famous Potato Salad, dill pickles, more Beach Boys, Kansas and Willie Nelson, and lots more family and neighbors.

Simple version

Potato Salad

Dice potatoes. Boil until firm (about 6 minutes)

Hard boil 6-8 eggs. Cut each into eight pieces, once cooled.

Dice a bit of onion (to taste)

Dice 6-8 kosher dill pickles.

Prep mayonnaise dressing, cut with a splash of milk and seasoned with salts, peppers, and perhaps a tsp or tbsp of yellow mustard. Blend with potatoes, eggs, pickles, onion. Chill.

Burgers

Season ground beef with Worcestershire or favorite steak sauce – approx 1 tbsp per pound. Form 6 patties from each lb of ground beef. Place cheese in the middle and pinch edges to contain the cheese while grilling. Reshape the patties and toss on the grill – about 5 minutes on the first side; 3 to 3 ½ minutes on the flip side for medium rare burgers with melted cheese.

Dress your buns; add burgers; add a beer; add tunes; collect friends.

Recipe for Success, with Freedom
Peeling the Allegory

Hamburgers (and yes, ok – grilled hot dogs) aren't as much metaphorical or allegorical as symbolic. The backyard grill-fest is a celebration. While I may enjoy the freedom to grill year 'round in Tampa, Florida, national prime cook-out season runs from Memorial Day through the 4th of July to Labor Day. These are reminders of *sacrifice, independence* and *hard work.*

The concept that "freedom is not free" is <u>not</u> over-done and applies well beyond the poignant return of flag-draped coffins from Iraq or Afghanistan. America's call for freedom in 1775 led eventually, through a war for independence from tyranny, to a Constitution in 1789. The first amendments to our Constitution: a Bill of Rights, ratified by the states in 1791.

People may lose focus on the fact that the Rights are owned by the People – not the government. But also, the *Bill of Responsibilities,* in the United States, does not exist, and instead is replaced by thousands upon thousands of local, state and federal laws, and the constabulary and courts to enforce them.

How does this fit into the task of teaching your junior leaders how to instill organizational patriotism in their subordinates? How, in other words, do we ensure both salaried and hourly employees aren't going to steal from the company, which includes shopping on the internet or updating social media during company hours, for example? If this is *not* a problem at your organization…an absolute zero problem…please give me a call.

First: Imagine any daily drive to work. You're approaching an intersection with stop lights and the signal turns yellow. You have enough time to stop safely before the light turns red. You could have punched the gas and made it part way through the intersection before the light turned red, but… You apply the brakes and come to a stop. Why did you stop?

a.) Because it's the law, or

b.) Because it's the safe thing to do?

What this gets to is the question of whether people are bound to the law – which gives humans infinite alternatives to find nuances around the fine points of the law, keeps attorneys in BMWs and fine wines, and adds to the millions of linear feet of case law and jurisprudence – or whether people (some people) actually do the right thing for the right reason.

Traffic signals and stop signs (laws) are a derivative of wanting to protect human life and personal property. If all drivers were focused on protecting human life and personal property, their own and someone else's, we wouldn't need stop signs.

Second: (The reader does not have to be Christian to understand the following concept:) In the Christian faith, a believer understands that he or she is not capable of faith through his or her own reason or strength, receives that gift of faith from the Holy Spirit of the triune God of the Christian faith, and believes that redemption of sins and the renewal or rebirth of eternal life has been purchased through the birth, teaching, death and resurrection of Jesus Christ.

That's a lot to chew on in this recipe, but whether you take it on faith or as an allegory…the question of the Judeo-Christian Ten Commandments comes up. "If I'm a good person and I don't kill, don't swear, don't commit adultery, don't covet my neighbor's ass…won't I get to heaven (*freedom from eternal damnation*) even if I don't believe in all that Jesus "mumbo jumbo?"

Well – no. All of that nice-to-have stuff, like stopping at stop lights and not coveting your neighbor's ass, or manservant or maidservant is roughly equivalent to *good works.* The concept in this second model is that "good works without faith….are empty." Faith comes first; good works are the result.

So. Allegorical or not – how do we teach our junior managers to instill an *internal* sense of organizational patriotism (faith) in our organizations, so they're not just punching the clock (showing up for "church") and going home without a commitment to the organization?

That company song comes to mind.

Symbols, rituals and myths define all cultures – even loosely organized anarchic organizations. People rally 'round flags, ideals, causes. The adage that there is strength in numbers holds true. What you need is an organizational propaganda. Just don't let the masses, who you seek to become psychologically unified, in on the secret recipe.

What follows? Back to the little girl at the Guest Quarters on the Navy base. One of the most powerful motivators for humans is the quest for a sense of relevance.

Marines on a mission rarely lack for a sense of individual and collective relevance. But even beyond combat or non-combat missions, they still seek recognition or acknowledgment – an awareness from their peers and seniors that they exist. Marines fight *first* for their brothers in arms.

And so – one of the most powerful tools at the disposal of a leader is the art of demonstrating to team members why their job (mission) is important and why *they* are important. A pat on the back, a smile, a personal note from a senior with a thank-you for a job well done are steps in the right direction.

Mission partly accomplished.

Marine Corps Leadership Principle:

Seek responsibility and accept it
for all that you or your team do or leave undone

Vol. 1 No. 8 **FOCUS** August 2005

Constant acceleration: an oxymoron?

Not too many Summer Olympics back, a woman sprinter replied to a sports reporter that she thought of her entire experience in a race – a matter of seconds – as *constant acceleration.* Acceleration is a change...in this case, a change in velocity.

So – what remains *constant*? Change? Isn't "constant" the same as "unchanging?" Isn't acceleration a change in velocity rather than constant velocity? Does all of this mean "constantly different?" I think there's more to it. We can think of constant acceleration or constant change in the same mind as *continuous improvement.* In fact, during the mid-1990's one of the flavors of the month in management philosophy was indeed Continuous Measurable Improvement – CMI.

I fell into this trap as a corporate contractor to General Motors back then. While GM was in the process of building today's cars with yesterday's technology, engineers in the back rooms were working on tomorrow's designs with today's technology – moving into virtual reality and math-based modeling and away from clay and balsa wood modeling, for example.

Yet the impetus to adopt Continuous Measurable Improvement bled into the non-engineering corners of the business as well. We were expected to develop *standard* practices for developing training materials, then improve them. Continuously. We were expected to develop a set of standards for interviewing new hire candidates, publish the standards, then change them. Constantly.

Seemed like a waste of time, honestly. Seemed like change for change sake. What if you *DO* get it right? How do you know? In the late 1600s and early 1700s, Italian master Antonio Stradivari apparently got it right. He and his sons set the gold standard for *both* the art and science of crafting violins and other stringed instruments – a standard that has survived more than 300 years.

Was Stradivari focused on Continuous Measurable Improvement? Actually...yes. For a while. The Academic American Encyclopedia tells us that Antonio Stradivari learned his craft "in the workshop of Nicolo Amati, whose family had been making violins for many years.

"After opening his own shop (1680), Antonio Stradivari *gradually* altered his violins, increasing their size by 1690; these longer instruments with flatter arches are known as the Long Pattern. About 1700, after further *experiments*, his violins achieved their mature state, and the next 20 years are known as the Golden Period. In those years, Stradivari made his finest violins, beautiful in appearance and sound and perfectly balanced."[xvii]

Once Stradivari found the right wood, the right chemistry, the right shape and the right processes – he stayed with it. Many have copied his models, and others have attempted to forge the Stradivarius, but what they did not copy or forge was what remained constant for Stradivari – passion for quality execution, and there is no logical sense in the idea of copying *change* or *improvement*. Companies change for change sake too often.

Back where we started? The answer may lie in the film: *The Last Samurai*. Tom Cruise, as "Civil War hero Capt. Nathan Algren, who comes to Japan to fight the Samurai and ends up pledging himself to their cause," is not "the last samurai." He is witnessing the last of the samurai.[xviii]

Algren and his former commanding officer travel to Japan as consultants to the Japanese, who seek to modernize and adopt Western ways of warfare. In the first skirmish between the ill-prepared government troops and the Samurai, Algren is wounded and taken prisoner by the Samurai. Recovering from his wounds and forced to adapt to his captors' way of life, Algren reflects, "What does it mean to be Samurai...and devote yourself, utterly, to a set of principles?"

Samurai? Devotion? Does that mean *samurai* is logically equivalent to the English word *disciple*? If we borrow this language and retrace our steps back to Stradivari, he would rightly be called, in his learning years, a disciple of Nicolo Amati. Later – a disciple of perfection.

In *The Last Samurai*, and in actual history, what the reform-minded advisors to the Emperor of Japan failed to realize was that in the process of changing to more modern ways of war, they lost their focus on the *constant* that had sustained the Japan of their history: service to the Emperor. The Bushido Code of the samurai. In a generation, the loss of the samurai would be their undoing. What remained of Bushido Code, ironically, sustained them into World War II, but that's another tale.

So now we are in the 21st century, surrounded by constant change. Some is driven by technology; some by changing social norms. Competition is no longer regional or national; in most industries – it's global. In business, if we don't change, or don't change fast enough, someone else in our industry will.

In all of this change, as disruptive as it commonly is, there must be some constant, something we can hang on to: the Olympic sprinter's constant, Stradivari's constant and the Samurai's constant. Cruise's Capt. Algren observes: "From the moment they wake, they devote themselves to the perfection of whatever they pursue. I have never seen such discipline" and "I am surprised to learn that *Samurai* means *to serve.*" Those of us who teach, lead, coach, manage or train junior members of our teams do so because we serve. As they become disciples of our tradecraft, together we seek *constant acceleration:* the relentless pursuit of perfection.

Recipe for Success, with Pork (spare) Ribs

A year 'round favorite...especially for weekend afternoons that can keep you busy, but close enough to the grill, for about three hours. If you have a cooling rack above the cooking surface, once you put the ribs on the grill, you only need to turn them once every ½ hour. With a 12- to 15-inch long rack of ribs, you may be tempted to surgically separate the individual ribs, but like your junior leaders entering their initial trials by fire, keeping them together has a purpose. This Perfect Ribs Theory starts with the same process for all three hypotheses: clean your kitchen sink with an anti-bacterial detergent and a dash of bleach. Rinse the sink thoroughly; then rinse your ribs using cold water. Rub thoroughly – to remove bacteria. Marinate in the refrigerator overnight and cook on low heat – about 250 on the grill – 2 ½ to 3 hours to an internal temperature of 140F (eliminates trichinosis bacteria).

Simple version

With a 9X14 baking dish (or suitable size pan or 1-gallon zipping-lock plastic bag):

Hypothesis 1:

Marinate generously with barbecue sauce.

Hypothesis 2: Marinate with teriyaki sauce. equally generously. Or...

Hypothesis 3: Spice rub: I use a bit of coarse ground pepper and a variety of seasoning salt spices, including garlic salt, all pre-mixed. Apply sparingly to all surfaces while the ribs are moist, after rinsing. Guests may wish to use barbecue sauce at the dinner table.

IMPORTANT!!! MARINATE OR RUB YESTERDAY!!! (and stow it in the fridge overnight).

Servings: 4 – 6

Prep Time: 10 minutes

Cooking Time: 2 ½ to 3 ½ hours (depending on the grill and heat settings)

Directions

Rib Fest Day is a Lynyrd Skynyrd day. Crank up *Sweet Home Alabama,* situate the ribs on the top rack/cooling rack, then crank up the grill – with two or three burners on low. The internal grill temp should reach about 250° F within 10 minutes. Set your timer to 30 minutes. Go mow the lawn. Return periodically (like – every 30 minutes) to turn the ribs. At 2 ½ hours – you can check the internal temp with a meat thermometer, or make a discreet cut with your pocket knife to ensure the meat is at least pink, not bloody red. If fixin's back in the cave are behind schedule – keep the ribs warm on the grill without over-cooking by cutting back to one burner.

Goes well with:

More Lynyrd Skynyrd, 4-5 guests, a pilsner or a pinot grigio, and a pile of potato salad (recipe in another chapter).

Peeling the allegory: from Convection to Convictions

Reassembling my favorite two-page newsletters from the past 10 years – I realize I must have had a temporary fascination with Social Entropy. Thermodynamics is a natural fit in the Grilling Studio; but social thermodynamics may seem a stretch.

What these hypotheses get to is my 2nd Law of Social Thermodynamics. In classical thermodynamics, the 2nd Law describes the tendency of a closed system (like a barbecue grill – roughly), with different pressures and temperatures, to move toward equilibrium over time. Turn *off* the gas to the grill and place a frozen rack of ribs on a grill with an internal temperature of 300° F; the internal temperature of the grill will drop. The rack of ribs will warm. Leave the ribs and the grill alone for a day – without a heat source and the entire "system" will reach equilibrium.

Thermodynamics tells us that this process is irreversible; it is impossible in this system to maintain the internal 300-degree temperature (with the grill lid closed) without an external heat source (defined as *work)* like propane and those 6 burners.

Social Entropy

Imagine, for example, you decide to start a new business – or even a new country. You surround yourself with four or five like-minded people. You're all the same age, so have a common (not necessarily identical) understanding of history; all of the same religion; same gender; same political persuasion; virtually identical academic credentials from the same university (all MBAs or all engineers for example). You all speak English as a primary language, hail from a common racial heritage and share similar tastes in music, culture, food and spirits.

You've surrounded yourself with yourself. You write a charter, or constitution, and all agree on your organization's vision, mission and goals.

But. Your company is so successful you eventually need to hire another full-time employee. Or, your country is so inviting – knocking at your country's door are some other country's "tired…poor… huddled masses yearning to breathe free, the wretched refuse of someone else's teeming shore." Try as you might, you can't find another clone; another You. Now what? Any negotiation on race, gender, age, academics, music, language, religion, politics or culture has the *potential* to dilute your organization's culture. Some will insist this will enrich your culture. That's part of the challenge. Again – the question is: what's *core* to your organization, your country?

If you're all men, and hire a woman – she might start angling for maternity leave. If you're all women, and hire a man – he might turn out to be a creep. If you're all conservatives and hire a liberal, you run the risk of Monday morning acrimony at the water cooler. If you're all middle age and your best qualified candidate is a teenager – you may have initial doubts about his or her work ethic…and he or she may have misgivings about your choices in music. People live by heuristics.

Our nation has absorbed those huddled masses for longer than we've been a nation. We even face the same general kinds of compromises in our marriages. What, exactly, is negotiable?

The theory of Social Entropy suggests that organizations expend enormous amounts of capital in maintaining their organizational cultures (acknowledging that change, once it has occurred, is irreversible without enormous expenditures of calories, capital or consternation). What is it they are *un*-willing to compromise on?

The lesson, through Pork Ribs on the Grill, comes from Social Psychology. The reason we keep those ribs together in their early leadership development is because, amongst all of the reasons humans justify their behavior (on or off the job), the realization that "everyone else is doing it" is one of the strongest. Military Psychological Operations (PSYOP), Religion, Education and Advertising all base their premises on the need to create, proselytize to and maintain a group of people who are *psychologically unified*. This is the core of the mechanics of propaganda.

(Don't worry about individual initiative. This is America. The Rugged Individual will always step forward.)

As you train your junior leaders, and as you teach them the fundamentals of creating Vision, Mission and Goals statements for your organization – lead them to William Bennett's *The Book of Virtues: A Treasury of Great Moral Stories;"* to the US Constitution's *Bill of Rights*, and to the *Ten Commandments* as teaching tools. Ask your junior leaders to consider the underlying meta-truths in these and similar documents. (What's wrong with "Thou shall not kill? Or Steal?" Almost every culture believes this.) Challenge them to reveal what they believe to be their own and their organizations' unbending values. If you find idealistic non-believers who think "Anything Goes" is the right way to go...think of this factual parable:

When my sons were about 12 and 14, they worked on convincing me that: "*Children* today (back then) are smarter, more capable and more sophisticated than their parents were at the same age." They believed this phenomenon was progressive and would drive the "age of maturity lower and lower." OK. They had access to the early days of the Internet. They had access to more television channels. They had access to more information. So I asked them: "Should I then eventually allow 10-year-olds to drive? Eight-year-olds? Should I expect six-year-olds to date and seven-year-olds to marry?"

The answer to the rhetorical questions about core values, above, is that we seek to maintain a set of organizational values while respecting individual cultural values. When individual values are destructive to an organization, it's not "diversity;" it's time for a pink slip. The reason we keep the ribs together is so that we can test them with a common fire. Their unity is reinforcing and convection builds conviction. Entropy is disorganization – and tautologically the opposite of organization. Your team members need conviction in values, reinforced by peers, to take on threats to the organization.

Marine Corps Leadership Principle:
Train Your People as a Team

Vol. 2 No. 7 **FOCUS** August 2006

Santa Factor and the alternate *jihad*

With Christmas a reasonably distant memory, August is a good month to take a breather and reflect on the correlation between bonuses, performance appraisals, Santa and *jihad*.

Correlate Santa and *jihad?*

<u>On Santa</u>

It's all about *human motivation.* In most corners of the world, children (including children who have no religious connection to Christmas) learn at an early age that "Santa, or an alias, like Pere Noel, Sinterklaas, Father Christmas, etc., is watching." Rumor has it Santa ties rewards to performance. Parents lead their children to believe that really good boys and girls get more presents... or bad boys and girls don't get anything at all. In Switzerland, we have a Santa Claus alter ego – known as Schmutzli in the German part of the country and Père Fouettard (from "whip") in French. The Swiss *Schmutzli* apparently collects bad children in a black bag and takes them back to the Black Forest or brings along a "broom of twigs for administering punishment to children whose behavior throughout the year has not been up to scratch..."[xix] (What a great concept for the HR Manager. *Schmutzli those non-performers!)*

This whole concept of passing around presents on holidays has (in my opinion) regrettably spilled over into Easter and Halloween. What's next – Columbus Day gift bags? Labor Day presents for the children? Arbor Day gift certificates? Presidents' Day surprises? The essence of this is the idea that if you are good, you are tangibly (financially) rewarded. The Santa Factor may or may not have some impact on children as they at least *try* to improve their manners in the weeks leading up to bonus (oops – I mean Christmas) time. But the incentive to perform is almost entirely extrinsic. (Motivations are internal; incentives are external.) The alternative – intrinsic reward – is superior.

Here's why: As leaders in our organizations, we have three tools to improve morale and respond to human needs (motivations). These are three types of rewards or *positive reinforcements*. The first of these falls into the category of *morale boosters*. Christmas parties, family picnics and free lunches are great morale boosters and can make your organization a fun place to work, but these events are not tied to productivity. Is there an organization out there anywhere that checks performance appraisal ratings at the door to the Christmas party?

Boost morale? Perhaps, but not much and not for long. Think of these morale boosters as *non-contingent reinforcement*. You don't have to do anything to get the reward, and everyone gets basically the same reward no matter how hard they work. Same thing with a McDonald's Happy Meal. Non-contingent reinforcement.

The second type of reward is your paycheck – direct compensation for work. In general, this *pay for performance*, an external, tangible reward, is a transaction. You punch in. You go to work. You get paid. But…you don't get paid second by second, minute by minute, hour by hour. There's no visible, tangible "hour glass" of gold dust at your work-station piling up your *compensation* as you earn it. Hourly or salaried, you typically don't see that reward but once every two weeks.

The guys who get paid to make up words for these ideas call the explanation for this experience: *expectancy theory*. The concept is that we work with the <u>expectation</u> that we will eventually receive that delayed compensation. It's delayed external, tangible reinforcement, postponed gratification…and it more than likely shows up as an ACH transaction in your virtual bank account rather than as gold coins in your pocket unless you visit an ATM. No doubt payday is an incentive to work. It responds to external motivations to own a home and buy food. It's just delayed.

<u>The Third Incentive</u>

The final option in incentives is best illustrated by considering your hobby: fishing, painting portraits in oil, paint ball, raising prize winning roses; deer hunting, collecting stamps or coins; rebuilding antique cars or clocks; running marathons; weight lifting; lovingly caring for your children or anything else that offers…(drum roll)…*Instant gratification.*

Ask 100 people how they feel about their jobs. Make a list. Then go to 100 other people and ask them to describe how their *hobbies* make them feel. With the notable exception of GOLF, the bet on the table is that most people will use <u>positive</u> (internal, emotional) <u>adjectives</u> and adverbs to describe their hobbies more so than their jobs. Most people likely experience the reward in a hobby internally, *especially while they are focused on their hobby*. Why is that? Instant positive reinforcement through internal <u>intangible</u> rewards is a longer-lasting and more effective motivator than external tangible rewards. Think *JOB SATISFACTION.*

Turns out there is a principle in the domain of Social Psychology to help understand this. Eliot Aronson's college text *The Social Animal* discusses the concept of *Justification Theory*, which builds on Leon Festinger's earlier work. At the core of this theory is the notion that we humans justify, or *rationalize*, what we do – particularly when we experience an internal (mental/ emotional) conflict. Aronson calls this *Cognitive Dissonance.*[xx] If I'm 9 years old and I'm being a good little boy on December 5th, totally against my nature (cognitive dissonance), I can justify it externally by the anticipation of lots of Christmas presents in a few weeks. But my good behavior likely won't last beyond December 26th. Or – I could justify it internally, believing that I truly *am* a good person. My reward is internal. I will probably be a good little boy all year long. This reward has a significant impact on my behavior. I have this internal struggle (cognitive dissonance) – be good, or be bad. Both have rewards.

On Jihad

It ain't just a holy war – as some in the world without Santa have co-opted the early use of the Arabic word. According to some Islamic scholars, it's an internal struggle – not a war. Not all Islamic scholars agree on this, but there is enough discussion on the topic in the blogosphere to open the dialog and make a comparison to Santa. One author notes:

This is an Arabic word which derives from the three-letter root j-h-d, which connotes "struggle," "striving," and "exertion." In the context of Islamic teachings, jihad refers to "striving for the sake of God." The word has rich implications and meaning, and has been employed in a variety of ways. In an everyday sense, jihad is understood by Muslims as each individual's effort to follow the teachings of Islam, to live a good and ethical life, to better oneself in the face of challenge or adversity, and to resist temptation or harmful inclinations. At no time did jihad refer to an effort to convert non-Muslims to Islam, nor was jihad seen in purely military terms. Consequently, jihad cannot be translated as "holy war."[xxi]

Either way – Santa or Jihad – the concept has been co-opted. The concept comes down to how individuals view their personal identity, their ontology. The internal struggle is over doing the right thing (for the right reason) when we are inclined to do the selfish thing. How well do you know your future leaders? Are they stuck in "a job" to meet someone else's expectations? What are their realities?

People learn to justify their performance through their leaders. You *cannot* motivate employees or children. Motivations are internal. Incentives are external. You *can* create an environment that leads to internal rewards for performance.

Adults in particular need to know how their performance contributes to that "something bigger than themselves." They seek relevance.

Recipe for Success, with Cloak & Dagger Thai Beef Salad

Ready in 1 hour 30 minutes

Ingredients

1 small head, romaine lettuce

1 small head, red leaf lettuce

1 Belgian endive

¾ cup olive oil

¼ cup fresh lime juice

3 tablespoons soy sauce

1 lb beef cut into strips

(The more tender the cut of beef, the more enjoyable the salad. You don't need tenderloin, but you could cut loose an extra buck or two for London Broil or Ribeye instead of flank steak.)

1 fresh gingerroot, grated (1" piece)

1 tablespoon brown sugar

2 cloves garlic, minced

3 jalapenos, minced

1/4 cup cilantro, chopped

3 tomatoes, wedged

2 green onions, chopped

Directions

Tear greens into bite-size pieces.

In small bowl, combine 2 tbsp each oil, lime juice, and soy sauce.

Add beef, stir, and marinate at least 1 hour at room temp.

In food processor, combine 1/2 cup oil, 2 Tbsp lime juice, 1 Tbsp soy sauce, ginger, brown sugar, garlic and jalapenos; puree.

Reserve marinade. Stir-fry beef in 2 Tbsp oil 'til just browned.

Mix reserved marinade with dressing.

Top greens with beef; pour dressing into wok and stir to heat and mix in beef juices.

Pour hot dressing over salad.

Add cilantro, tomatoes, and green onions; toss.

Serves 4

Ice down eight bottles of Thai beer.

Recipe for Success, with the *concept* of Jihad

It's an artifact of history that Marines (like other travelers) have picked up words and phrases in their global expeditions. One alternate moniker for Marines, for example: *Devil Dogs*...is storied to have been applied to US Marines by their German Army opponents in World War I. Marines returned from Vietnam in the 1960s and early '70s with *didi-maow* (let's get the hell outta here!) and *baow chi!* (don't shoot!). Today, when senior officers travel to Washington DC to brief the generals, it's not uncommon to hear reference to a *shura* (from the Arabic – in Iraq) or *jirga* (from the Pashto in Afghanistan)... in reference to a senior council.

Jihad is another of those terms that has gained a foothold in the vernacular of Marine conversation, as in: "I'm gonna wage a little jihad upside your head if you mess this thing up." But as noted in the essay that opens this chapter, *jihad* has at least two meanings: the ostensible *war* in defense of a particular version of a religion, and the "struggle in the way of Allah" in order to live a good and righteous life.

Since we cannot see inside our team members' hearts and minds, we are left with theories of human motivation – which abound in the world of personal and social psychology. We can observe behavior and question our team members in order to draw inferences about why they are willing to go off to war or drive in to work day after day...but one thing we cannot do is motivate them.

Another term Marines have picked up over the years is *Gung Ho*. Major Evans Carlson led World War II Marine Commandos in the Pacific – Carlson's Raiders. Carlson borrowed the term "gung ho" (work together) from the Chinese Industrial Cooperatives moving supplies in the resistance movement against wartime Japan. In time, for Carlson, this anglicized version meant "work together – *with enthusiasm*." Thus, Marines who are enthusiastic are (or at least used to be) described as Gung Ho. (There is more to this story, but this gets the point across.)

Like the rest of us, Carlson was internally motivated. Incentives are external. If you think about it for a moment…the men and women who served in World War II – many away from home for three years or more – as well as those who served in Vietnam, or Korea, Iraq or Afghanistan…didn't really see a paycheck. They weren't browsing the new cars at the dealership; going to the hamburger joint or coffee shop. External incentives became delayed gratification and compensation. Most of them did not think in terms of getting home to their saved pay (it wasn't much in 1945 anyway), but to their wives, girlfriends and families. And yet they "showed up for work" on a daily basis.

So what else is there besides external (financial) incentives and internal (often very personal) motivations? Major Evans Carlson was *gung ho* – enthusiastic – to the point of being inspirational. The histories of his Marines attest to this. If you don't have trust in your leaders, enthusiasm for your mission – even if your mission is a profit-focused or service-oriented mission – you can't expect your team members to wage jihad for any other incentive than cash.

Marine Corps Leadership Trait: **Enthusiasm**

What's the symbolism in Thai Beef Salad? An Internet search reveals countless recipes for this concoction. It may be served as a side – as a salad – or as a light meal with a crust of bread and a Thai beer. The title suggests this is Thai BEEF salad, not CILANTRO salad or GARLIC salad or ENDIVE salad. It's the cut of beef that makes the difference, that inspires the taste buds. We may not be able to motivate our team members, but we can certainly *inspire* them. Inspirational enthusiasm can be infectious and *fire up* your team members. You actually *can* pay a couple of dollars more and buy tenderloin, and ensure when you "stir fry" the beef you're not destroying the meat. So let's be real: I'm not going to spend $12 to $18 per pound for strips of beef to garnish a Thai Beef Salad seven days a week, but when I *do* make the salad and add it to a special dinner, I'm also not going to toss 75% lean hamburger on a pile of lettuce and call it "thai beef salad." We're looking for inspiration here, Boys and Girls.

Where does that leave us? If you have "motivational speakers" addressing employees, and your employees leave the motivational speaker experience feeling "enthusiastic," they have to answer for themselves *why* they are enthused. Because the motivational speaker is? That's crap. That won't last any longer than the speaker's rented Chevy sits in your company's guest parking spot. Every member of your team deserves to be seasoned with the organization's mission and how their individual missions contribute.

Without purpose, the mission becomes the paycheck.

Vol. 1 No. 3 **FOCUS** March 2005

Beware the I'ds of March (& April & May & June &...)

One of the role-play exercises we pick up on the final day of our Leadership seminars is:

If I were CEO for a day, I'd...

While some participants take the cynical view: *"I'm not going to stick my neck out; I'll never be the CEO,"* our goal is to get people thinking along the lines of taking the risks of leadership.

The contrary example that comes to mind is the 1958 comedy film *No Time for Sergeants*, in which good ol' Andy Griffith gets drafted. As hayseed Pvt. Stockdale, Griffith is assigned duties as the Permanent Latrine Orderly (The PLO)(before there was a "Palestine Liberation Organization"). This dubious position is akin to the euphemistic "sanitation engineer," or the kid who doesn't get picked for either team in a sandlot baseball game. (You get to be "All-time Catcher.")[xxii]

Being *all-time catcher* doesn't seem like a lot of fun. Being a *sanitation engineer,* and picking up other people's garbage doesn't either. Yet the baseball game becomes mystically dysfunctional without a catcher...And as for the garbage, you'd have to be in your 40s (at least) to remember the impact of the 3-month sanitation worker strike in New York City back in the 1970s. This adventure made the nightly news in the Walter Cronkite era, when the city center became a landfill, with all of the rats and smells that come with it, and the mayor calling in the National Guard and declaring a state of emergency.

Who's got leverage now? (If I were the Mayor of New York, I'd...)

But this isn't about leverage, it's about *ownership*. Now – back to the movie: Andy Griffith's character is painfully naïve and literal, which leads to the most humorous scenes in the film – including Pvt. Stockdale taking the *initiative* to create a system that makes the toilet seats "stand at attention" when Stockdale presents the latrine for inspection. Where is the leadership lesson in toilet humor? Ownership leads to Initiative.

But you don't *own* the company? Maybe not, but you own your job. And you alone are responsible for your future. Consider this: If your job is replaced by technology; if your entire department or even entire plant is replaced by offshore workers in another country – who is responsible for getting *you* your next job? Who will hold your hand to get you into college or training for the next career?

The *only* person who will create a future that YOU find satisfactory is you. Which brings us back to "If I were CEO for a day, I'd..."

Well, you are CEO. You are the CEO of *you*. If you find elements of your job to be inefficient – document them and bring them up to your manager, director or VP. If you don't work in a culture that embraces innovation and recommendations for change, stuff those recommendations in the Suggestion Box anonymously. Daily.

No one's going to listen to you? Remember Lech Walesa, President of Poland from 1990 to 1995? From 1961 to 1965, Walesa was a car mechanic. He then served two years in the Polish Army and in 1967 started work as an electrician in the Gdansk Shipyards. Twenty-two years later, in November 1989, as the elected President of Poland, Walesa became the third civilian in history, after the Marquis de Lafayette and Winston Churchill, to address a joint session of the United States Congress. Something happened in those 22 years of Walesa's life – something important enough for him to speak up.[xxiii]

The question is: *How important* is it to you? What are you willing to risk?

If I were CEO, I'd...but time gets away from me. I'm so busy with the spouse, the kids, and the commute, and drive-through windows and...Apparently *initiative* requires more than urgency and ownership (decisiveness); initiative needs time.

"Will you marry me?" takes two seconds. (What's the risk vs reward?)

Classroom time for a master's degree takes about 25,000 to 30,000 minutes. (Risk vs. reward?)

A 4-hour marathon, at about 9 minutes per mile, takes 240 minutes. (Risk vs. reward?)

Time? Beware the "I'd take initiative – if only I had more time." In three years there are roughly 1.5 million minutes. You likely sleep a third of that (8 hours out of 24 hours a day). That means you're awake about a million minutes every three years. If you're the typical American working 2080 hours in a year, that's 124,800 minutes. Multiply

2080 hours X60 minutes X3 years and you get 374,400 minutes. Where *do* those other 625,000 minutes go…while you're awake but not *on the clock*?

You *own* those minutes. Your life and your job are your *enterprise*, which happens to be the root word in *entrepreneur:* A person who organizes, operates, and assumes the risk for a business venture.

As CEO for the day, I *will*…rearrange time, weigh the risk and take the initiative.

Recipe for Success, with Fried Rice

(Beef Fried Rice, pictured; with Veggie Stir Fry: cabbage, mushrooms, onion, zucchini and yellow squash)

Prep Time: 40 Minutes

Cook Time: 22 minutes – Rice; Stir Fry – 5 more minutes

Ready in: 1 hour

Servings: 6-8

Tunes: Fleetwood Mac

Brew: A German or Dutch beer (iced)

Ingredients

1 cup long-grain, enriched, white rice

2 cups water

2 eggs

12-ounce package peas & carrots, frozen

Soy Sauce

Olive oil (or peanut oil, or canola oil)

Directions

Prepare 1 cup "scratch" rice with 2 cups water. Bring water to boil; pour in one cup of long grain white rice. Reduce heat to lowest setting and set timer for 22 minutes – unless you're at a different altitude in Golden, Colorado or somewhere in Tibet. Then – I have no idea.

While the rice is cooking, work on one of the other questionable recipes in this book, or something safer – like Sudoku.

When the rice is done, turn off stove and remove the rice from the heated surface. Let sit for 2 minutes.

Prepare a 12-inch skillet or wok: Pour two tablespoons oil and two tablespoons soy sauce in skillet. Set burner to high. When the soy sauce sputters in the olive oil, the oil is hot. Add the rice.

Fry rice, blending rice thoroughly with soy and oil. Browned rice is okay, but don't overcook.

Add two raw eggs. Toss.

Add vegetables. Toss until vegetables are hot. Don't overcook.

Fried Rice is endlessly flexible. With nuggets of beef, pork, shrimp or other ingredients, it's easily a meal in itself. As a side, Fried Rice goes well with shish kebab and other mains, and this combination can be used (with variations) as the stuffing for cabbage rolls and stuffed peppers.

Recipe for Success, with The Standard Deviate

Or: Recipe for Disaster – with Success

Before launching a fried rice metaphor (or any other recipe) incorporating the anthropology of leadership and organizational dynamics, let's agree that the primary difference between the two is that the ingredients in your rice recipe are essentially inert and that (most) humans are individually and collectively both chaotic, and complex-adaptive, living systems.

Individually chaotic and complex-adaptive? Perhaps in pairs. Individually – we *are* entropy and tend through a process of decay to inevitable destruction. At least in pairs we retain the promise of moving our genetic code a bit further along the emerging path of adaptive systems.

This view, however, depends on how far one is willing to view an individual organism as a self-organizing system: The human organism has sensitive dependence on initial conditions (genetics), is responsive to a changing (random) external environment, develops within a set of rules – so is deterministic, but not predictable, and so on. (But without X's and Y's getting together, we tend to disintegrate at around 80 years on average. And some of the humans on your team may seem inert from time to time.)

Meanwhile, the link, of course, is the leader – as chef, orchestrator, choreographer, guide, master…The world offers an unlimited array of drinks, fruits, vegetables, meats and spices; an increasingly diverse range of options in how to prepare them; and more blending and *fusion* of previously sequestered flavors – like "Mexican" and "Chinese" (which in the US are likely neither originally Mexican nor Chinese). For leader and grill-master – it's chef's choice.

Consider Six Sigma in a McDonald's, Burger King or Wendy's environment. The global restaurant chain's goal – at least within the boundaries of the US market – is that every burger or sandwich from Maine to Hawaii is substantially identical. With "lots and lots served," a traveler from Maine, on vacation in Hawaii, can typically expect his sandwich to look, smell, feel and taste pretty much identical to the sandwich he's used to in Maine.

Six Sigma-like quality in a restaurant suggests errors in sandwich making should be on the order of one in a million...six standard deviations. (As noted in the introduction to this book, find that Malcom Gladwell YouTube video discussing Moscowitz and Ragu versus Prego spaghetti sauces.)

That look/touch/smell/taste familiarity is an essential element – a mathematically predictable element – in the (Six Sigma-like) quality of this restaurant-kind of enterprise. But even a top-end Steak House restaurant, where Mr. and Mrs. on their 1st Anniversary might expect to spend $200 for a dinner for two – relies on standardization. Even *their* product, from state to state, is essentially identical.

Not so at my grill. Hypotheses for dinner for all!

What about that recipe thing for leaders?

Complex Systems in Business and Terrorism

Theorists and writers have applied both Complex Adaptive Systems Theory and the parent Chaos Theory to studies in leadership, management and complex organizations (like private sector businesses) in countless books and monographs. Viewing al Qaida and its violent extremist adherents in this light – as a business – individual terrorist cells, and indeed individuals, respond (adapt to) changing external environments, take in information from their own like-minded adherents, from the broader ummah (the notional "nation" of Islam), and from a variety of external positive and negative feedback sources.

Collectively, al Qaida's adversaries – including the US and partner nation armed forces and a range of US and other nations' government agencies – adapt as well. The challenge for *both* is to stay one step ahead of an enemy in tactics, techniques and procedures until there is an inevitable defeat of one or the other. The alternative is a festering generations-long state of conflict. (That's where we are today: a festering generations-long state of conflict.)

What we take from this in the private sector is an understanding that al Qaida and its adherent organizations have morphed (adapted) into profit centers, with significant cash flows from kidnapping for ransom, smuggling weapons and drugs, trafficking and smuggling humans, counterfeiting, extortion and the other typical mafia-like activities required to keep a business in business. (American businesses, as profit centers, generally tend to avoid kidnapping for ransom as a way to keep cash on hand.)

What's the point? Two things.

First: We likely won't see al Qaida, the Taliban, Boko Haram (in Nigeria), Lashkar e-Tayiba (in Pakistan), or AQ's franchises in North Africa or Yemen applying for ISO-9000 certification or Six Sigma quality banners over their favorite hang-outs. They measure their "quality" by a different set of standards, but they measure it nonetheless. (Are you really thinking about this?) Al-Qaida and AQ-related franchises have a measureable impact on all businesses in America, including business travel, taxes, security, and the decline in consumer confidence across a range of industries – which impact a range of *other* industries.

Second: While terrorist organizations may *quantify* their successes – just as the US and other armed forces do – there is one quantifiable certainty: it is exceedingly difficult to predict *individual* human behavior. We may try to predict where specific attacks will occur – in Iraq, Afghanistan or elsewhere – but the best we can do is understand broad motivations and we rarely predict, accurately, where the next attacks will occur. Likewise – we can predict that X number of people will buy a particular computer or smart phone today...or Y number of people will buy a logo shirt and some groovy jeans at the high-end retailer at the mall (and the truth of this knowledge is in the "same store sales" demands on retail store managers) – we just don't know *which* customers will buy these products on a daily basis.

Take all of this randomness to Six Sigma quality and ISO 9000 programs. After two decades of working with a wide variety of mostly private sector organizations moving into or sustaining one quality certification or another – every one of them, without fail, was focused on the math (profit), the statistics. But – many of these organizations won their ISO 9000 (or 9001) certifications and soon found that a significant "percentage" of their employees went back to business as usual. The quality mongers in these organizations failed, or didn't know how, to account for the human terrain…social psychology outside of statistics. Why? Social Psychology is too hard. Can't quantify it. Engineers run the company. People are un-predictable.

OK.

Really?

Then don't hire any "people" if they're so unpredictable.

(Again: Are you *thinking* about this?)

Learn People.

People are fractals. People run into and respond to strange attractors. Humans in the 6th standard deviation – Standard Deviates – are endlessly flexible and unpredictable at the extreme of one in a million (six sigma or six standard deviations), and it only takes one… to wreak havoc. The best we can do is predict human performance, or motivation, in the aggregate. But we *can* understand human motivations. And we *can* understand people.)

Fried Rice – a bit more predictable.

BOTTOM LINE

ISO 9000 and Six Sigma certifications are awarded to organizations, not people. As we train junior leaders, it is not the people we seek to standardize, nor even their stores of knowledge – but the core *values* of the organization.

Marine Corps Leadership Traits:
Decisiveness; Initiative

Vol. 3 No. 7 **FOCUS** July 2007

Marginalizing
the office Smart Donkey

Like many (I suppose), I've had my share of run-ins with the guy or gal who always seems to have a comment that he (or she) thinks is clever – but actually serves as a put-down…or who spouts language that belongs in a sewer. The comment illustrates that he can't think of something intelligent to say, and serves to make himself look good by way of making someone else look bad. He lacks the ability to rise above his meager standards, so he makes his meager standards seem higher by attempting to make others lower.

Although there are endless offenders who are not truly all that bright, the worst offenders seem to be those who are rather intelligent. They also have the potential to be the most dangerous, the most stinging, acerbic, caustic, biting wits in the cubicle maze or on the plant floor. Their command of the language avails them of a wider range of vile, stupid things to say – often exacerbated by the use of foul language seasoned with four-letter words.

When we complain, and the boss (or someone else) says…"That's just the way ol' Dave is," this response is *unacceptable*. Accepting a donkey's standard for acceptable language or behavior means that we have bent to *his* wishes, his lower standards. He's not a joker, a clown or a comedian. He's a controller.

A *controller*.

Make no mistake – we *all* attempt to control and rearrange the world around us. We get a sense of freedom by feeling *in control*. When we let the federal government take control of our lives – we are forsaking freedom. We all seek to define what we wear, whom we date and marry, what our home looks like inside and out, the relative comfort of our clothes, homes and cars, our jobs and our friends. We select, arrange, rearrange and de-select all of these and more on a fairly regular basis. That much is human nature.

Think of it as redecorating. Most redecorating is an attempt to *control* our environment to suit our personal needs. No problem. But most of us negotiate realistically. When it's time to redecorate the garage, we may *want* a new sports car but we settle for the minivan – that has more room and gets better gas mileage.

The Donkey is not negotiating. This experience is reminiscent of a summer of camping with three 9-year-olds – all precocious and extraordinarily literate for their age. They can pun; they can sling sarcasm; they can play with words all day long. They know how to dish it out; they just lack the maturity to take it back. Nine-year-olds generally aren't that good at diplomacy and negotiating, and diplomacy and negotiating are the arts of give and take.

Stretch the metaphor.

In the global game of negotiating, for example, the North Koreans give up a nuclear power plant and take, in return, 500,000 metric tons of oil or half a million bushels of wheat for their failing economy and starving 20 million people. The negotiator's goal is to get North Korea to abide by a world standard in nuclear non-proliferation. (And then the

North Koreans announce they are well on the way to building nuclear weapons anyway.)

Again – allowing someone with lower standards to determine the standard is unacceptable. Whether the weapons are nuclear or verbal, the gold standard must meet the test of "best for the common good." This works for manufacturing, global logistics, medicine, aerospace, energy, higher education – or Iraq, Iran, Afghanistan, or the floor of the U.S. Senate and House of Representatives. We think of this as *civil* behavior. The behavior of U.S. Senators and Representatives is no textbook for our children's understanding of civil behavior or language. The filthy, hideous, unacceptable examples of numerous Congressmen and women, of certain US Senators, should be worthy of jail time and fines.

What passes for *civil* admittedly evolves over time. The bawdy public language in use during William Shakespeare's time, 400 years ago, fell into disuse in the 17th and 18th Centuries as men and women of letters reformed governments and fought colonial oligarchies with strong but carefully worded language. (Get into *The Federalist Papers.*) That doesn't mean the coarse language disappeared – it merely went underground to "the locker room" or the saloon.

Stretch the metaphor again.

Because they have no choice, in asymmetric warfare, what we call terrorists are labeled *freedom fighters* by others. The United Nations has yet to come to terms with an internationally accepted definition of terrorism. In parallel, the U.S. Congress and Supreme Court have yet to come to terms with definitions of pornography and what constitutes *acceptable language* in public venues. What used to be unacceptable has, in a generation, moved from the underground back into broadcast media...and back into the office. Everybody's concerned about *their* First Amendment rights with little or no concern for someone else's right to not have to listen to it.

In the 1960's, comedian George Carlin had a routine called "The 7 Words You Can't Say on Television." He didn't say these words on television – the gig came on an LP record. (Yeah – I know, you almost had to be around in the 60's to know what an LP is...) But it was a decision to buy or not buy the record. Now the cautious consumer of electronic entertainment has to decide to block or not block, listen or not listen to a radio station or television channel. The workplace doesn't even offer that level of freedom. Smart Donkey comments are often spontaneously out-of-place and to avoid listening to them *could* mean quitting your job.

What to do?

Censor and Censure: Putting great value in my small role in support and defense of the U.S. Constitution (against all enemies, foreign and domestic), I ascribe to the tenets of The Bill of Rights, and especially Freedom of Speech. I'm a writer. I survive on freedom of expression. Remember when dress codes relaxed in the 1990's?...and some people ruined it for the rest of us by showing up for work in tank tops and flip flops? Organizations then had to respond to that lack of responsibility with specific dress codes. I want to write whatever I want to write...I don't want limits, but I believe I have responsibilities.

Rules.

In combat, the Geneva Convention and Rules of Engagement (ROE) serve as a guide in the chaotic environment that requires judgment and decision-making.

Businessplace ROE – for language – may work, sometimes. The question is:

"Is the foul language necessary to accomplish the business mission?"

If not, get rid of it.

Psychology suggests that you could avoid responding – denying the sort of reinforcement that fuels the Donkey. (If you allow it, you reinforce it.) This requires an enormous effort, to not merely avoid responding to the Donkey's inappropriate comments, but avoiding the Donkey altogether. Donkey is also the beast who's usually complaining about the way we run our business, undermining leadership, defeating or deflating morale. Donkey likely also creates a measurable, negative financial impact on the bottom line.

Alienate, ostracize and marginalize the Donkey. Convince your co-workers to guarantee the Donkey has his own pasture – where no one steps in Donkey's filth but Donkey.

Recipe for Success, with Calf Liver

As the Office Donkey's language and demeanor are distasteful, it seems appropriate to give a nod to the tender bit of calf liver – on the grill.

Ingredients

4 packages ramen noodles, generally in a plastic bag. Cost – typically 15 to 50 cents each. Toss out the little packet with 1095mg of sodium and 12g of fat

1 lb packages of frozen carrots, cauliflower or edamame – to taste

6 oz jar mushrooms, drained.

1 tsp sea salt

Protein: If you feel a need to add a "meat" to your noodles, cube chicken breast or shrimp (small, bite-size pieces), and boil with the veggies; add to the noodles.

Directions

Start water and sea salt boiling. Add veggies and boil for 2 min. Place dry ramen noodles in large soup bowls. Ladle enough boiling water into each bowl to completely cover the noodles. Add portions of vegetables (and chicken or shrimp) on top of the noodles (and a splash of soy sauce, if desired).

Cover with an inverted bowl or plate for 2-3 min. Enjoy.

We like to add stir fry veggies with a lobster tail or prawns (on the grill) – pictured.

Truth

If the reader *still* feels an uncontrollable urge to actually eat calf's liver…wait until your neighbors have left for their once-a-month Friday or Saturday date night. Sneak into your neighbor's back yard and fire up *his* grill. Toss a pound of the distasteful organ on a hot grill, bottom rack, for 10-12 minutes on a side. Grill it to shoe-leather consistency.

Done. Saute some fresh mushrooms and sliced onion in extra virgin olive oil and soy sauce. Add to the liver, and wash down with a non-descript light beer. Don't forget to turn off thy neighbor's grill. (My family served liver two or three times a month when I was a kid. Mom said she liked it. I think it was a step toward easing the budget for a family of seven. It's an acquired taste. I never acquired the taste. If the goal was to cut the budget – and be thankful for what we had – Lakeway Manor "Chili" with ramen noodles was all we needed.)

Recipe for Success, with Civics

Peeling the Allegory

During those first years of monthly Leadership and Conflict Management seminars, and living on ramen noodles, I had the occasion to make a graphic point for my workshop participants about differences of opinion. In advance of a conflict management workshop, I spray-painted black a ¼-inch thick plywood disk (about the size of George Carlin's vinyl LP), drilled a hole in the center and inserted a rod…an axle…long enough for a first volunteer to hold the rod and spin the disk. (On both sides of the black disk I had painted a white, silver dollar-size circle as a reference point.)

Two additional volunteers took positions, with one standing <u>behind</u> the volunteer with the disk, the other <u>in front of</u> the first volunteer – both facing the disk. On request, the first volunteer spins the disk, slowly, and we ask the other two participants if the disk is turning clockwise or counter-clockwise.

Despite watching exactly the same phenomenon at exactly the same time, the witnesses were unable to reach an agreement…

…other than to agree: *It depends on how you look at it.*

This sophomoric example replicates the Coriolis Effect and the fascination of youngsters in learning that water retreating in flushing North American toilets exits in a clockwise spiral while Australian toilets flush counter-clockwise. So – human behavior may be described as something like:

$$\mathbf{\Omega} \times \mathbf{v} = \begin{vmatrix} i & j & k \\ \Omega_x & \Omega_y & \Omega_z \\ v_x & v_y & v_z \end{vmatrix} = \begin{pmatrix} \Omega_y v_z - \Omega_z v_y \\ \Omega_z v_x - \Omega_x v_z \\ \Omega_x v_y - \Omega_y v_x \end{pmatrix}$$

(Kind of a *Hitchhiker's Guide to the Galaxy* explanation for unacceptable behavior…) So if Coriolis Force is a result or consequence of Inertia (see Newton's 2nd Law), what we're dealing with in the Office Donkey is *the lack of an inclination to motion, exertion or change.* We want to <u>change</u> that distasteful behavior. At least I do.

One of most disappointing examples of this trend assaulted my auditory sensibilities while serving in Iraq in 2006-'07. Returning to active duty at the age of 50, and deploying to Camp Fallujah with an Intelligence Battalion at the age of 51, I was three times older than the youngest Marines in the Corps. We didn't have any 17-year-olds in the battalion I deployed with, however, so I was only 2.68 times older than the 19-year-olds in that battalion. *That* was comforting. I was only 2.68 times removed from what was considered acceptable demeanor, 2.68 times more old-fashioned. All but one of the nearly 20 enlisted women Marines serving in the battalion were younger than my grown sons, in their 30s. Most of these women Marines swore like drunk sailors on a port call – All day long, while conducting daily business, 15 to 18 hours a day.

If they wanted to fit in with "the guys" – they did. If they wanted to establish the lower limits of civil behavior and re-define the upper limits based on *their* foul language – they did. And when the officers and senior non-commissioned officers (all men but one) both failed to prevent the foul language and used it freely themselves…they reinforced and rewarded the lower limits.

The words *civic* and *civil* come from common Latin roots – related to the concept of citizenship. This problem of civil language: in Fallujah with my fellow Marines, on television and radio, in stores, offices and manufacturing plants across the country, on the floors of the House of Representatives and US Senate…is a <u>leadership</u> problem.

Look up the word *palindrome.*

In terms of leadership responsibility, the word CIVIC is the same word – no matter what side you stand on.

Marine Corps Leadership Traits: **Bearing, Tact**

Marine Corps Leadership Principle: **Set the example**

Conclusions

As I pulled together the Leadership essays which supply the core this book's message, my intent was to learn how to format books for publication – first in e-books, then in print. My longer-range goal is to retire into publishing… someday.

What I discovered is that I am once again a student. If I want to learn the business, I have to accept there is more to this job than just having an English degree. I am therefore indebted to those who teach portions of the business, and in teaching – pass on building blocks of knowledge, ingredients in the cookbook of "how to be a publisher." I'm thankful for the age of the internet with unlimited tutorials in Adobe's Photoshop and Illustrator, in Microsoft's Office products, user forums, blogs and much more.

Because I seek to be a leading independent publisher (and not just a *self-published author*) I am wrapping up a Master's in Entrepreneurship at the University of South Florida. This not only affords one the opportunity to learn business planning, strategic market assessment, new product development and a half-dozen other key sub-disciplines, but also provides access to amazing library services. Most fascinating in this process is engaging with knowledgeable professors and fellow students who are half my age. Wicked smart people they are.

On the front end of this adventure, I found the kind of business I wished to model: Greenleaf Book Group based in

Austin, TX. I learned the story of Founder and CEO Clint Greenleaf at the Self-Publishing Book Expo in Manhattan (selfpubbook expo.com) through Mr. Greenleaf's Chief Operating Officer, who was one of the presenters at the expo. I like the model, and better yet – the story, because it's a model of independent entrepreneurship and hard work. From the Greenleaf "About Us:"

Clint Greenleaf started Greenleaf Book Group in 1997 after he graduated from college. During that summer, before he started as a staff accountant at Deloitte, he wrote a book called Attention to Detail: A Gentleman's Guide to Appearance. *Despite being written as a joke for his friends, it proved to be successful by filling a need in the market. Clint developed a passion for publishing and retired from Deloitte after all of seven months at age 22.*

Well done, Clint and team!

———

Meanwhile, this story is done and I have something burning on the grill.

Comments? E-mail me at:

karl@vademecumpublishing.com

i From Wikipedia: http://en.wikipedia.org/wiki/Enron. Accessed 7 Jun 2012. Enron Corporation was an American energy, commodities, and services company based in Houston, Texas. Before its bankruptcy on December 2, 2001, Enron employed approximately 20,000 staff and was one of the world's leading electricity, natural gas, communications, and pulp and paper companies, with claimed revenues of nearly $101 billion in 2000. *Fortune* named Enron "America's Most Innovative Company" for six consecutive years. At the end of 2001, it was revealed that its reported financial condition was sustained substantially by institutionalized, systematic, and creatively planned accounting fraud, known as the "Enron scandal". Enron has since become a popular symbol of willful corporate fraud and corruption.

ii Connors, Roger; Smith, Tom; and Hickman, Craig. *The oz principle: getting results through individual & organizational accountability.* Portfolio, 2004. Initial publication: *The OZ Principle,* Connors, Smith & Hickman, 1994; Prentice Hall Press.

iii Wikipedia: Semi-permeable membrane. Accessed 12 June 2011.

iv IPA is short for "India Pale Ale," and refers to a class of pale ales… *India pale ale* is a yardstick for the class.

v Howell, William. © 2011. http://alaskanbeer.blogspot.com/ Personal correspondence: 14 June 2011. Please conduct an exhaustive web search to see Bill's accolades as 2010 Beer Drinker of the Year, read Bill's weekly blog, vote for his continued success, and savor Bill's weekly advice in the Alaskan beer blogspot.

vi Homeowners lost 55% of their housing wealth, more than $7 trillion when the housing bubble burst and House and Senate Democrats and Republicans refused to compromise on solutions. http://articles.marketwatch.com/2011-07-08/commentary/30711408_1_middle-class-wealth-housing-bubble. Retrieved 20 July, 2011.

vii Estimates of the measurable impact of 9/11 approach $2 trillion. http://www.iags.org/costof911.html. Retrieved 20 July, 2011.

viii An excellent read is: *Being Wrong: Adventures in the Margin of Error* (© 2010 Kathryn Schulz), Harper Collins, NY

ix (whatis.techtarget.com/ definition/0,,sid9_gci759332,00.html (via AskJeeves.Com April 1, 2005)

[x] *Stuck in the Middle with You.* By Joe Egan and Gerry Rafferty and performed by their band Stealers Wheel, peaking in 1973, on Stealers Wheel, at #6 in the U.S. Billboard Hot 100 chart.

[xi] Gomez, J. *The Assessments Process in Contemporary Operating Environment.* Smallwarsjournal.com. June 22, 2011. © Small Wars Foundation.

[xii] Drucker, P. *The Essential Drucker:* Chapter 5, Social Impacts and Social Problems. P. 58. Harper. 2001.

[xiii] Collins, J. *Good to Great.* HarperCollins. © 2001 by Jim Collins.

[xiv] http://www.aerlines.nl/issue_26/Knol_SWA.pdf, retrieved 7 Aug 2011.

[xv] http://pewresearch.org/pubs/2111/veterans-post-911-wars-iraq-afghanistan-civilian-military-veterans

[xvi] 1980, Association Press. ISBN 0695814729

[xvii] "Stradivarius" in the Academic American Encyclopedia © 1989 by Grolier, Inc. Danbury, CT.

[xviii] *The Last Samurai* © 2003 Warner Bros Entertainment. Directed by Edward Zwick.

[xix] (http://www.swissinfo.ch/eng/Home/Archive/Schmutzli:_the_ Swiss_ Santas_sinister_sidekick.html?cid=7082046).

[xx] Aronson, E. *The Social Animal* (5th Ed.), W. H. Freeman and Company, 1988.

[xxi] (http://www.theislamproject.org/education/Prepare_eval.htm.(12 Feb. 2006.)

[xxii] *No Time For Sergeants.* Based on the Mac Hyman Novel. Directed by Mervyn LeRoy. Warner Bros. 1958.

[xxiii] Lech Walesa info retrieved March 9, 2005, from: http://nobelprize.org/peace/laureates/1983/walesa-bio.html.

www.ingramcontent.com/pod-product-compliance
Lightning Source LLC
Chambersburg PA
CBHW060026210326
41520CB00009B/1011